PROCLAMATION BY DESIGN

The Visual Arts in Worship

Karmen Krahn and Leslie James

To Lonelle,
[signature]
1/05/08

Faith & Life Resources

Scottdale, Pa.
Waterloo, Ont.

Library of Congress Cataloging-in-Publication Data

Krahn, Karmen, 1971-
  Proclamation by design : the visual arts in worship / by Karmen Krahn and Leslie James.
      p. cm.
  Includes bibliographical references.
  ISBN-13: 978-0-8361-9402-9 (pbk.)
  1. Christianity and the arts. 2. Liturgics. 3. Public worship—Audio-visual aids. I. James, Leslie, 1951- II. Title.
  BR115.A8K73 2007
  246—dc22
                                   2007043137

Unless otherwise noted, Scripture text is quoted, with permission, from the New Revised Standard Version,
©1989, Division of Christian Education of the National Council of Churches of Christ in the United States
of America.

The publication of this book was made possible through funding from Mennonite Church USA and the
Schowalter Foundation.

Library of Congress Control Number: 2007043137

International Standard Book Number: 978-0-8361-9402-9

Cover and book design by Gwen M. Stamm

Cover images: details from two of seven banners designed by Bob Regier, North Newton, Kansas, for the First
Mennonite Church of Hillsboro, Kansas. Banners were quilted by a team of women from the congregation.
Photography by Designer Images, Hillsboro, Kansas.

Printed in Canada

Orders and information:
USA: 800-245-7894
Canada: 800-631-6535
www.mpn.net

Table of Contents

Foreword

This is the book for which many pastors and churches have been waiting. In a time when the lively role of the visual arts in worship is being rediscovered, we need a trustworthy guide to help us navigate this colorful new landscape.

Here is what often happens: Some well-intentioned person decides the worship space needs a little decorating. A bouquet of flowers here or a cluster of candles there brightens the space. Before long, however, such persons discover that the urge to decorate has a far deeper source and much greater potential. As they hear Scripture proclaimed and sung in worship, they become aware of a growing desire to bring the Word to life in visible form.

In church traditions that have offered little guidance for this transition from decorator to illuminator/interpreter of Scripture, many congregations stumble. How do the visual arts faithfully proclaim the Word? How do they express the congregation's theological commitments? How does visual art become integrated with other elements of worship? How do artists receive feedback that will help them learn and grow? Who assists them in practical issues of scale, appropriate materials, and finances? And finally, where do these folks store all the "stuff" needed to fulfill their call?

Proclamation by Design offers thoughtful, tested guidance for each of these questions and many more. Among resources for visual arts in worship, it is unique in its focus on Scripture as the organizing center of worship. Karmen Krahn and Leslie James gracefully articulate a theology of worship and give plenty of practical guidance—everything from organizing a liturgical closet to cleaning up spilled wax. They make clear connections among the congregation's encounter with God, its life together, and its mission in the world.

I am especially grateful for the binational partnership that made this book possible. Following in the tradition of our denomination's publication of hymnals and curriculum, Karmen and Leslie collaborated from their respective locations in Saskatchewan and Kansas, working tirelessly and against great personal odds to complete the project. Their vision and commitment are evidence of God's grace and the Spirit's renewing energy. To each of them I am personally grateful. And in time to come, churches that use this resource will also be profoundly grateful for the enlivening worship it inspires.

Proclamation by Design offers a vision that the postmodern church needs. At the heart of Christian faith is the Incarnate Word, which every Christian is called to embody in daily life. This book will equip the church to experience the Word-made-flesh in worship, thereby inviting worshippers to see and taste and touch the glory of God and to be transformed to love and serve Christ in the world. I commend this book with great joy!

—*Marlene Kropf*
  Denominational Minister of Worship (Mennonite Church USA)
  and Associate Professor of Spiritual Formation and Worship
  (Associated Mennonite Biblical Seminary)

Acknowledgments

This book is the product of a long journey of collaboration among Mennonite leaders and congregations across North America. Following a consultation of publishers and educators in January of 2001, a group gathered to discuss the creation of a congregational worship resource on the visual arts in worship. In November of the same year, Mary Lou Weaver Houser, Leslie James, Karmen Krahn, Michael Yoder, and Pamela Bressler Yoder met in Indiana with Marlene Kropf, Minister of Worship for Mennonite Church USA, to work further on a proposal. Karmen was affirmed as the principal writer for the project, with Leslie as collaborator.

In 2004 we received a green light from Mennonite Publishing Network to develop a manuscript. We interviewed worship leaders and visual artists in several locations in the United States and Canada, and we integrated our findings and photographs into this book. We obviously could not contact every Mennonite church, and we are sure that we missed some wonderful examples of the arts in local congregations. Eventually, over two years, we collected stories and photos from nine states and four provinces (see page 142).

We wish to thank the following artists, pastors, and congregational representatives who responded so graciously to our queries: Dorothy Dick, Esther Kreider Eash, Joanna Fenton Friesen, Matt Friesen, Todd Friesen, Carol Sue Hobbs, Michelle L. Hofer, Vicki Hofer-Holdeman, Mary Lou Weaver Houser, Norma Johnson, Joe Loganbill, Doug Luginbill, Eric Massanari, Jane Peifer, Barbara Peterson, Joanna Pinkerton, Chuck Regier, Elsie Rempel, Frances Ringenberg, Deb Schmidt, LaVerle Schrag, Kris Shenk, Lois Siemens, Randall Spaulding, Pauline Steinmann, Lavina Thiessen, Mark Wasser, Tonya Ramer Wenger, Lynette Wiebe, and Laurie Yoder.

This project also would not have been possible without the generous financial support of the former Mennonite Board of Congregational Ministries (for meeting expenses) and the Schowalter Foundation (for photography and travel expenses).

An immense debt of gratitude goes to our editor, Byron Rempel-Burkholder, who helped us form an unwieldy and often untamed manuscript into the book you hold in your hands.

We also offer special thanks to Marlene Kropf of Mennonite Church USA and Eleanor Snyder of Mennonite Publishing Network for their patient and faithful shepherding of this project to fruition. Finally, to all those unnamed loved ones, friends, and colleagues who, even on the most unendurable days, endured us, encouraged us, brought us coffee and chocolate, and continue to speak to us in spite of it all, we offer our deepest appreciation and gratitude.

—*KK and LJ*

Introduction

In the concentric circles of congregational life, worship is at the center. Contrary to the configuration of most pews, this is the shape of worship. Worship is a promised presence, for where two or three are gathered, there God has promised to be. What we say and touch and see in that presence is of vital importance to our growth in faith, our formation in community, and our corporate witness to the world. Worship is a response to what God has done and continues to do. And it is in worship that we are formed into a people shaped as, attuned to, and participating in God's activity in the world.

"Be thou my vision," we sing, understanding from Jesus' many parables and healings that vision is a cardinal metaphor for faith, and that faith is the beginning of having our lives transformed. "God be in my eyes and in my looking," we pray, understanding that the world looks profoundly different when we see it through God's eyes. Set within the context of corporate prayer and Scripture, glimpses of God's intended kingdom form that motivating set of images toward which we move. Images of salvation from both testaments erase the boundaries between worship and mission and the sluggishness that befalls us between Sunday and Monday. What we see in worship becomes the goal of Christian service. What we experience in worship shapes us as the people of God.

There is a long history in Protestant worship of creating formative images primarily through words and music. Certainly these are important avenues. The Word is broken open through the words of the sermon and reflected in the prayers of the gathered body. The singing of God's praises, enjoined by the Psalms, is a dearly held tradition of Protestant worship. At the same time, Protestants have been reluctant to use visual images in worship and, at some junctures of their history, have even prohibited them. Spaces of simple design and empty walls have long been a hallmark of Mennonite meeting places. Yet even in such surroundings, the visual has spoken. The centrality of the pulpit has spoken to the importance of the proclamation of the Word. The height and openness of the space has spoken of the vastness of God. Plain windows, creating frames for sky and trees and fields, have invited reflection on the beauty and wonder of God's creative energies.

As we move further into the twenty-first century, into what is being called the postmodern age, the visual and the experiential are coming to the fore—not as replacements for the spoken word, or for the voices raised in praise, or even for accepted symbols of pulpit or worship space, but as additional and vital avenues for the proclamation of the good news of Jesus Christ and the formation of God's people. The intentional introduction of the arts has the same purpose as that of preaching or hymn-singing—to proclaim the Word of God. The focus of this book is the proclamation of the Word of God through the art and arts of worship in our assemblies. We hope to offer both foundational and practical help for integrating the arts into worship.

We begin with a "Call to Twenty-first Century Worship," a brief statement reflecting our time and location, our opportunity and responsibility, for the proclamation of the gospel early in the postmodern age. To talk about faith as Christians is to talk about belief in God revealed through Jesus, the risen Christ, who is still in our midst by the Spirit. In a postmodern, post-Christendom world, we must remember that what we see shapes us; what we gaze upon affects our vantage point; and that upon which we meditate and in whose company we pray guides our worldview. Worship, at the center of Christian life, formation, and witness, is where this happens.

The book is then divided into three main sections—a series of foundational essays, a catalogue of color photos, and a set of hands-on ideas and helps. The first section is called "The Gallery." Imagine walking into a large, metropolitan art museum. Once inside the door, we are invited to begin a journey through rooms of art, each focusing on a particular period, artist or theme. Exploring each exhibit builds our understanding, and we leave the museum ready to reflect on the ways in which all that we have seen is interrelated. There are four such rooms in our gallery. The first considers the God we praise; the second, the Scripture we proclaim; the third, the design we offer; and the fourth, the people we become.

Next is a catalogue of art created for worship in particular congregations for a particular service or series. When we enter a gallery in the museum, we are not met simply by a description, but by actual works of art that embody the period or artist or theme. The art brings the theory to life and makes the visit truly memorable. The art is not offered as pattern to copy, but as illustration and inspiration.

Finally, in "The Studio," we will find tools and work spaces for creating art for worship. At the start of an art class, students are invited to tour the studio in order to become familiar with available materials, to locate the tools for good composition, and to become familiar with both good technique and safe handling of materials and tools. A thorough tour of the "studio" in this book will allow us to become familiar with the materials in the closet; to look at the design, interpretative, and evaluative tools that can help guide our work and build our confidence; and to take special note of the suggestions regarding safety and good technique. Following the initial tour, feel free to use the studio as your own. Dig in, with heart and soul, with mind and hands. May the God of all colors bless and keep you. May the faces of God shine upon you and be gracious to you. May God's full palette be revealed to you and give you joy.

The art created in this studio is meant to be an integral part of congregational worship. It does not exist as a monument to itself, but to serve the God we praise, to proclaim the good news of Jesus Christ, and to highlight the work of the Spirit in forming God's people. In the end, the arts in worship are offered to God in the company of worshippers in much the same way first fruits and the first-born were brought to the temple. May God do with them as God will. May they lead us to pray and wonder, to praise and confess. May the God we praise use the Scripture we proclaim, through the design we offer, to form the people we become.

—*Karmen Krahn*
  Leslie James
  Season of Epiphany, 2007

A Call to Twenty-first Century Worship

To the worshipping church postmodern people are saying, "Grant us . . ."

a place of gathering

If Jesus, the risen Christ, plays the role of host
    then visual art shall adorn the Host's front door.
    It is a banquet table lovingly set with the nourishing Word.
It need not (and ought not) always be beautiful,
    only spirited and true. Welcome to worship.

a wordless sanctuary

Wordless evocative biblical art is its own call to worship.
    Where modernity has been criticized as "long-winded,"
        postmodern worship is refreshingly light on words.
        Wordlessness is pastoral care.

So, if the Christ candle is lit upon entry we need wait for no verbal cue.
Christ is here. Let us pray.

an engaging mystery

What science did in modernity in helping us understand
    the mysteries of the universe,
the arts are doing now in helping us encounter the mysteries of God.

Science peers through a microscope.
Worship peers through prayer—
    offering a glimpse of strangers becoming friends,
        granting access to new and surprising faces of God,
            imagining the kingdom as Jesus did.

a story intricately woven

One Sunday at a time the worship leader becomes a story weaver.
    The warp is strung beforehand—Scripture below, prayer above,
    ritual below, songs above—round and round til Sunday comes.
Using the shuttle of imagination, the worship leader sends
    the *individual* story through the weave of *corporate* story until the two
        become part of the entire tapestry of salvation history.

The tapestry is only finished at the time of the benediction.

imaginative license

Visual art in worship is not an artistic luxury. It is ethically imperative,
    for if moral, spiritual, and mental transformation begin with
        imagining new ways of being, we cannot worship without it.
Peace-making begins when we imagine what peace looks like
    according to God's original design. We do this in worship.
Forgiveness and hope are not so much doctrinal propositions
    as they are mind-expanding ways of seeing.

room and reason to participate

Visual art is a prompt and a permit to move.
    "Still life" was never meant to sit still. In the hands of people
    the church's symbols come to life in the most dramatic visual design of all.
    God's people abandoned in praise is at once worship and mission—
        for what more does God desire?

What could be more attractive to the watching world?
Modern worship sat. Postmodern worship moves.

a new calendar

The modern calendar has left people tired, scared, overwhelmed and broke.
As colorful and symbol-rich as its cultural counterpart,
the Christian calendar allows us to locate ourselves in time marked
by banners, not sticky notes. Color, not credit cards.
Candles, not headlights and symbols beyond the computer's toolbar.
Here, we find icons of transcendent meaning and eternal value.

a new clock

By design, modern clocks tick in electrical silence.
By design, liturgical clocks tick audibly in chimes
and colors and loud hosannas. What time is it? "He is risen!"
By design, modern clocks are sharp and angular, glowing red.
By design, the theological clock is round and welcoming,
coming around again and again with annual symbols of deliverance.
Modern clocks are alarming; the biblical clock is motivating.
We carry modern time with us on our wrists;
biblical time transports us in memory and hope.
By design, modern clocks tick without ceasing. This is a falsehood.
God's clock, by design, reminds the church of rest, renewal
and ultimate fulfillment. This is true.

a trustworthy ritual path

Full-being encounter with mystery in Jesus Christ.
Entered into together, experience of community, imagining a new way of being.
Environment in which the Spirit is given space and time
to act and do as the Spirit of God would choose,
transforming messy, clumsy rehearsal

into distinctive, revolutionary reality.
Envisioning the completeness of the Kingdom of God
    amidst the already and the not yet.

liturgical freedom

The church is a body of freewill participants.
    May the art be corporately made, claimed, and interpreted.
The church's worship is public.
    May the art be relevant, rich enough in meaning for all who gather.
The church worships with intelligence, willfulness, and virtue.
    May the art be free of cliché, propaganda, and moralistic prescription.
The church gathers freely in joy and thanksgiving.
    May the art inspire us to confess and relive ongoing suffering.
The church gathers freely in suffering and despair.
    May the art remind us that reconciliation is the hope God wants us to
    see.

an acknowledgment of reality

For the worship leader as prophet—the visionary, passionate truth-speaker—
    evocative art serves as an act of solidarity, of pastoral care.
For the gathered, looking to see God, evocative art invites them to
    revelation, an experience of God.

        And so,

Seeing ourselves rightly, we confess and repent.
Seeing the world more justly, we are motivated for mission.
Seeing ourselves with undeserved proximity to God's holiness, we praise.

The Gallery

liturgical freedom

an acknowledgment
of reality

room and reason
to participate

a trustworthy
ritual path

imaginative license

a story intricately woven

a new calendar

a new clock

a place of gathering

a wordless sanctuary

an engaging mystery

Chapter 1

The God We Praise

I think God is invisible but then, God's pretty tangible in other ways. We don't actually see God, but we can see that God has a tangible plan. Or, there are things we recognize that we turn into tangible things—like the attributes of God, ways we have experienced God, the goodness of God. It's just the concept that's invisible. There are things we know about God and those very things are available for show. You work with the invisible God by making tangible your epiphanies and experiences. —LaVerle Schrag

Invisible. We come to this page with our eyes wide open, yet we are only able to talk and write about the God we praise. The praise we bring, apart from our best attempts to describe it, remains an offering to a God who is unseen. Words, written or spoken, endeavor to do just what visual art does through the eye: describe God to the imagination. So indispensable is the religious imagination that we can go to worship singing "God is here among us" without a second thought.

Imagination in reference to God belongs to that part of the brain where belief comes to life in exquisite pictures. These pictures are companions to a story that Christians love to repeat when the church is gathered with God alone at its center. God's story, God's primacy, and God's people—these are the essentials of worship. We gather to praise because, week by week, we profess belief in a God who still makes appearances. Our faith lies in the Creator unseen and still worthy of praise, in Jesus ascended and guiding the church from a 2000 year-old story, and in the Holy Spirit indwelling, as visible as our next act of compassion.

A theologian is anyone fervent in the search for "evidence of things unseen" in God's plan: God's attributes in Christ, epiphanies, and experiences of the Holy Spirit. This generous definition of a theologian includes all believers, not just preachers and seminarians, in the ongoing labor of making God known. Theology is a word that will be used throughout this book and will be understood to mean, simply, an awareness of God's presence. If your eyes are open and you expect to see God, you're doing theology.

With one eye trained on God's next appearance and another for fine art, LaVerle Schrag

The arts draw us deeply into the parts of ourselves where our most urgent questions and desires lodge. These desiring questions have as their source and end, God.

—*Wendy M. Wright*
Weavings

Revelation is not a matter of thinking or feeling, intuiting or sensing . . . It is a shocking gift of new sight that obliterates such distinctions, grabbing us by the lapels and turning us around, so that when we are set back down again we see everything from a new angle.

— *Barbara Brown Taylor*
  The Preaching Life

uses the term "turning" to describe the work of such theology. As an artist of faith, she will not talk about art destined for worship before talking about God. She also cannot talk about God without somehow referencing Scripture. An artist of faith "turns" into medium what has come through revelation[1]—converting the invisible into a visible commentary. That medium is seen not only privately but communally, and not in general strokes, but in the fine detail of whatever medium suits for telling the Story of God.

Every artist has a medium for this "turning" task—notes for music, words for speech, worship objects to handle with the eyes and hands. Since their beginnings in the Reformation, Protestant churches have grown to appreciate these media, outfitting each one with special furniture—a solid set of pews with pockets for the hymnal, a solid, centralized pulpit with amplification, and a solid communion table bearing the most sacred symbols. Pulpit, pew, and table are the worship easels upon which our praise sits. They are the places our senses go on a quest for the proclaimed word, searching for images lodge in faith's imagination.

The furnishings of Protestant worship spaces indicate the priority of Scripture—heard, seen, and sung. At Superb Mennonite Church in central Saskatchewan, the pulpit, pew, and piano occupy the same visual plane, none more prominent than another. The pulpit proclaims in preaching what the piano evokes in singing from the stories of Scripture, which lies open and bookmarked on the communion table. Worshippers expect proclamation from any furnishing where leaders of song and word turn into art what is found in revelation.

Not long into a conversation about art, artists like LaVerle tend to wander back to these places of theological origin. Their eyes are open and they expect to see God. Gratefully, they find that the God we praise has chosen to be tangible in countless ways throughout the story. Artists, eager to bear witness in their preferred medium, seem to revel in this. In burning bush, pillar of fire, tempest, and deafening silence—God is here among us. Seen high on a mountain and in dove descending, with thunderous voice and in the cry of a newborn—God is here among us; let us all adore. When we know the unseen God to be among us, we have encountered revelation. Theology is the search for God; revelation is the finding.

God converses with Abraham, seals the lips of Zechariah, reveals heaven's splendor to John. As the biblical story shows, worship is a conversation of responses and revelations, all at God's initiative. It is a conversation in testaments, Old, New—and newest (our story today). Psalms, the anthology of Israel's worship conversation, is the design of a covenant people who rightly expect God to show up. The "face of God" is Hebrew code language in a community that knows intimately the visibility of God. The face of God, everywhere apparent in Hebrew experience and story, is reflected in the lavish temple built to worship God.

When your church talks about God's presence, what cherished vocabulary does it use? When your church tells of God's presence, which metaphors, images, and symbols accompany the story? It behooves every leader to learn this code language of congregational words and images in describing God's presence, absence, and disposition.

The term *theology* is our shorthand for what we know of God, our experiences with God, and our understanding of God's ultimate movement. Theology lies at the root of our worship. Our eyes are open and we expect to see God. Theology shows up in the words prayed and sung, and in the spaces where we gather to blend our voices.

From here, the big coat of theology gets a snugger fit, tailored for the more particular discussion of *worship* theology. "The God we praise" is a discussion of worship theology. The underlying notion of our specifically *Anabaptist* theology of worship is that what we do together shapes who we become together. Worship, done together, with God at its center through the story of Scripture, is the most formative activity the church can do. We are people of the Word.

Theology is the search for God; revelation is the finding.

In Trinity

Indivisible. The invisible God, unseen but everywhere visible, is also the God self-revealed in Scripture to live in indivisible community. Since the early days of the church, the church has used the term *Trinity* to describe this unity. The word simply means that something is threefold, that it exists *in* three. It is a way of describing the God who lives as community, three in one, and who lives in community, one in three.[2]

The dynamism of God as one in three and three in one is often reflected visually. One longstanding symbol of the Trinity is the triangle. Three sides join at three distinct points, creating stability while also illustrating equal and continuous interaction along the lines and between the points. Another ancient image for Trinity is found in the Celtic knot, which joins three distinct, equal, and interlocking loops and for which there is neither beginning nor ending.

If we think about such images just a moment, it quickly becomes clear to us that, as people of the Word, we simply cannot discuss God without talking about God revealed in human flesh through Jesus Christ, or about the Holy Spirit indwelling God's people. There are many ways to characterize these distinct manifestations of God. Here are some rich images for our imaginations to explore:

The church's central task is an imaginative one. By that I do not mean a fanciful or fictional task, but one in which the human capacity to imagine—to form mental pictures of the self, the neighbor, the world, the future, to envision new realities—is both engaged and transformed.

—*Barbara Brown Taylor*
   The Preaching Life

God as creator and source—the one whom we love and praise with heart,
mind, body, and soul
God as Christ, brother and redeemer—the one we follow as disciples
through death to resurrection
God as Spirit and energy, animator of our world—the one who empowers
us to witness and serve with joy[3]

The opening words of Genesis introduce us to God, the Creator, revealing the master artist, shaping and forming, working in broad strokes and intricate detail, establishing contrasts and creating symbols. As the story unfolds, God is revealed as intimately engaged in creation, as the sustaining source of life.

The opening words of the Gospel of John reveal God taking on human flesh and dwelling among us. Jesus' life and ministry are the visible manifestation of God and God's Kingdom, the perfect pairing of revelation and design. What we know of God, we know most fully in Jesus Christ. Jesus, in fact, introduces the Holy Spirit as God's empowering presence in the communal life of his followers (John 14:26). This Spirit fires our imagination to recognize God, the Creator and Source, and enables us to offer praise with all our being. And the Spirit guides and emboldens us to live into the life and character of Christ, to become the people of God.

The Trinity matters in our life together. It gives us an operational truth for our life together in the church. God's very being exists in community, and community is relational. God's history from walking with Adam and Eve in the garden, to leading the Hebrews to the promised land, to Jesus taking on human flesh, to the Spirit being sent as guide—all moves toward drawing us, too, into community. The Trinity suggests images of our lives in and before God. Thinking of God in Trinity, we can begin to imagine and understand ourselves as:

Body, mind, spirit.
Created, redeemed, led.

We can think of our ways of knowing as:

Intellect, senses, emotions.
Imagination, conscience, relationship.

As the people of God, then, we find ourselves:

Seeing as God sees.
Loving as Jesus loves.
Behaving as the Spirit leads.

The trinity should be the pattern of our unity.

— Richard Sibbes,
17th century theologian

Created in the image of God, we are molded to live out of and into trinitarian ways of being a community that God has brought together. We are to seek the good of the community. We are to work for justice, healing, and wholeness. Within our congregations we take on differing roles and exercise differing gifts, thus making visible the Kingdom of God. We are many and we are one. We are distinct, yet we are formed into the indivisible Body of Christ.

The underlying assumption of Anabaptist worship theology is that what we do together shapes who we become together. Worship, done together with God at its center through the story of Scripture, is the most formative activity of the church. In worship we work through our revelations of the triune God. We give form to our response, and then open ourselves to further revelation and response. We are people of the Word becoming the people of God.

Trinitarian Worship Design

If our theology consists of what we know of God, our experiences with God, and our understanding of God's ultimate movement—how do we "turn" this invisible revelation to the communal commentary and expressions of praise we offer in worship?

This conversation can begin and remain grounded through a simple, yet eloquent, visual cue of threeness, using the stuff of our common life to remind us of God:

> *As a stumped artist I often return to the foundations of our faith and most often that foundational image is the Trinity . . . three candles, three colors of cloth, or combinations of three like a plant, a rock, and a Christ candle. Our congregation knows that when we see an assemblage of three, we'll be praying to or singing about God in the Spirit, in the name of Jesus Christ.*[4]

Recalling that theology has to do with having our eyes open, expecting to see God, and that God revealed is the root of our worship—how do we understand Trinitarian worship and worship design?

In God as Creator, worship is an encounter of mutual abiding. God is the agent of covenant in whom we find our identity as people of grace. We find God's agenda revealed in the grand narrative of Scripture. We take on that story. It becomes our perspective. In the communion of worship where our glad response meets God's initiative, we say to each other, "I know you." It is here that doctrine works itself out through God's actions in creation; in ongoing, mutual relationship; in holy, perfect, preserving, faithful, and redemptive love. Through this encounter of mutual abiding, God's is the vantage point through which we look into ourselves and out into the world.

How can we invite our imaginations into dialogue with the revelation of mutual abiding? Consider this image of God's arms outstretched and reaching out to God's people:

> *Take a long piece of dark blue sateen. Fold it in half. At the halfway point, attach a strand of fishing line and suspend the sateen from the rafters, rising eight feet from the floor. Take two microphone stands. Remove the mics and squash a four-inch Styrofoam ball at the top of each one. Drape one side of the suspended fabric over each foam ball, discretely securing the pins. Allow the fabric to fall in two deep swoops. The remaining fabric will naturally conceal the microphone stands. These are the outstretched arms of God.*

In Jesus Christ, worship is an encounter of mutual adoration. Jesus is the agent of radical obedience in whom we find our identity. We find Jesus' agenda revealed in his behavior. In the communion of worship where our glad response meets his initiative, we say to each other, "I love you and I am willing to die for that love." It is here that the church talks about the moral demands of Christian living. Love, obedience, and sacrifice form the axis of discipleship. Jesus' preaching, teaching, and healing provide the lens through which we view and respond in the world. In this encounter of mutual adoration, we take on Jesus' character as our communal virtue.

The following formative memory of imagination illustrates our invitation into dialogue with the revelation:

> *When I was probably five, my dad would preach in the church in Hamburg, Germany. Children, they said, were not allowed. And, yet, my mom wanted to go to church. . . . We'd sneak up to the organ loft where . . . I would lie down on the floor by the organ pedals and look up. The church had a domed ceiling and on this dome was a painting of Jesus, a huge Jesus with his arms outstretched on the clouds . . . We'd lie there really quietly, looking up at that beautiful ceiling. . . . That memory is burned into my head: seeing Jesus, hearing my dad's voice go up and down. . . . Then one day, when I was all grown up, we returned to Germany and to this church . . . I wanted to see Jesus. I looked up at the ceiling . . . and it was beige. I was devastated . . . . I'm sure the paint was peeling off when I was five, but those were such a formative set of experiences.[5]*

In the Spirit, worship is an encounter of mutual summons. The Spirit is the agent in whom we find our ecclesial identity. We find the Spirit's agenda in the sustenance of the church's call. That vocation becomes our mission, regardless of our individual occupations. In the communion of worship where our glad response meets the Spirit's initiative, we say to each other, "I need you." It is here that the church talks about mission and its relationship to the world. The Spirit, the gift of God's indwelling presence, continues to teach, to remind, to guide, and to empower. Through this encounter of mutual summons, we are shaped and sent.

Consider this example of imagination being invited into dialogue with the revelation of mutual summons.

> *In the season of Ordinary Time, a worshipping assembly gathers each week under wispy, yet clear, reminders of the gifts of the Spirit enumerated in 1 Corinthians 12 floating weightlessly over their heads across the entire worship space. Months later, upon seeing a photo taken during that series, many in the assembly raise their heads, seeing again in their mind's eye that which had fired their imaginations in summons and given form to vocation.[6]*

With eyes wide open, expecting to see God, these windows into the triune God, drawn from our common life, carry within them a compelling invitation to the imagination. Words, spoken or on a page, simply cannot hold or express all the revelations of the Word among us, unseen but everywhere visible. "The truth of Christianity is not found in words, but in Jesus Christ—the Word made flesh, God's living image."[7] Revelation and insight come, as does God among us, through all of our senses and bids us respond with our whole being. A fitting call to worship that is sufficient for any church expecting God to show up: "Come and see."[8] God says, "Come!" Art says, "See!"

The biblical account is minimal. There are so many invitations to the imagination.

—*Bruce C. Birch*
Arts, Theology and the Church:
New Intersections

Theological Imagination

Theological imagination is about what things look like. It's about seeing into reality, discovering how the strange and extraordinary pieces of our stories fit into the strange and extraordinary pieces of God's story. It's about taking another look. It's about listening for layers of truth in what's before our very eyes.[9]

Inexhaustible. We can never run short of opportunities to see God if our eyes are wide open. We will never come to the end of our revelations of the God we praise. Imagination, that essential trait of the Creator so richly imprinted within each of us, is likewise an inexhaustible tool for the work of theology. Lest we doubt the validity of imagination in this work, consider the use of image in the Scriptures. The psalmist takes us to green pastures, to roaring oceans, or into a universe whose wonders are ever more visible through the Hubble telescope. In his habitual telling of parables, Jesus paints word pictures that ask us to fill in the details, discover new meanings, and bring the Word "home," into their very lives. Or observe the Spirit taking the form of tongues of flame, igniting the hearts of those gathered on Pentecost. As people of the Word, committed as we are to Scripture, such accounts are clearly invitations to imagine.[10]

> Lent began one year with incomprehensible layers of black scrim. As the weeks moved along, the layers became less overwhelming and, though still shrouded, a vague hint that something lay behind them began to emerge. Easter Sunday the assembly gathered to discover the remaining scrim rent top to bottom, though what lay behind remained a mystery. Then, at the proclamation that Christ was risen indeed, the scrim fell away revealing a gloriously colorful, abstract sunburst, a collage of torn tissue paper on a net backing that invited the natural light behind it to illuminate it even more fully. Nothing literal, not even representational, but a jumping off point for Easter imaginings, resurrection possibilities, a face of God revealed.

"With that piece," says artist Esther Krieder Eash, "I am instantly reminded of warmth and welcoming and all these words we use to describe a welcoming God."

It is easy for us, 2000 years out and knowing that the end of the story is not crucifixion but resurrection, to march right past the disciples' grief and despair as they approach the tomb on that first Easter. We know that we are gathering to celebrate, so we easily overlook the fear that must have pervaded each heart. The Story is pulled forward to meet and mix with our story, however, as we enter a worship space that still holds the sense of emptiness that the death of a loved one brings, the heartbreak of dreams dashed by tragedy, or the fear that accompanies an altered and uncertain future.

Now, with our stories quickened and our wounds exposed, we are prepared to approach the tomb with those first visitors and receive with them the news that Christ is risen. We are ready to capture a sense of that joy, to imagine not just what it must have been like, but to begin imagining what it *is* like now, whatever our circumstance. We can imagine the welcoming face of God, color breaking through the greyness and sunlight rushing in to warm and illuminate the darkest corners of our experience. Alleluias, no longer merely words on a page, rise from the very soles of our feet to express the very depth of our souls, a full-being response to the God we praise.

Imagining Anew

All this talk about imagination, art, and full-being response may seem intriguing, perhaps even exciting to us, but it may not square with our history and experience in the church. For many of us in our growing up years, the Word was proclaimed in the sermon and the people's response was limited to praise sung in unison or in four-part harmony. Walls were often stark, windows clear, the worship space purely functional. This austerity, or some variation of it, was part of the Protestant understanding of faithfulness from the early days of the Reformation.

So why all this discussion of imagination and the arts as integral tools for theological work and for expressions of revelation? Most simply, in the early days of the 21st century we find ourselves in a very different place than did our ancestors in the 16th century. An oft-heard term that can help us quickly grasp some of these important shifts is *postmodernism*.

Today, countless books grapple with what the postmodern world looks like. There is even debate about whether or not we have fully arrived in the postmodern world or, perhaps, have settled into what academics call a "transmodern" world. What is not being debated, however, is that a major shift has occurred. The privileged place that knowledge occupied when the Enlightenment gave birth to the modern era has broken down. Truths that science once held to be immutable have been repeatedly blown open to reveal deeper mysteries instead of hard, rational fact, prompting postmoderns to call into question things that were once considered absolutes. Much of this questioning stems from the fact that the cultures of the world are being brought together through technology, commerce, and travel.

The ripple effects of this shift have profound implications for the church. Postmodern people ask, "Can there be one Grand Narrative that should be privileged over others?" Today, different demands are made of the stories that guided the lives of earlier generations. Whereas the modern would ask for rational proof of the existence of God, the postmodern seeks experience with God. Whereas moderns often expected all fellow worshippers to understand and to believe in a lockstep manner, postmoderns live with questions and with diversity in understanding; they hold paradox and mystery as central to the experience of faith. Whereas a reason-dominated modern was apt to compartmentalize Sunday worship

Many have come from . . . frugal no-nonsense churches who had no desire and saw no need to light candles, hang fabric, meditate on an icon, or use rocks, sand, shells, water, or twigs to illustrate a Scripture text. We deeply appreciate our heritage with its simplicity and love of song, word, and fellowship. But many of us found something lacking in our worship—the use of visual beauty and sacred symbol.

— *Randall Spaulding*
Sarasota, Florida

from the workweek, the postmodern seeks a holistic faith that is lived out in everyday life without drawing divisions between secular and sacred. The postmodern world challenges the church to be "real," that is, holistic in its practice, communion and mission and own up to the truth that God is beyond rational explanation—or else God is not God.

Our Reformation ancestors lived in Christendom—a world that for centuries had been called Christian, not necessarily as a matter of faith, but more often as a reality of citizenship, taxation, and education. While the Reformation movement addressed these issues, the privileged place of Christianity as the narrative that guided society continued in Europe and then North America. Well into the 20th century, the privileged status of Christianity began to break down. Those of us old enough to be reading this page were alive at the functional end of Christendom.

The world in which we now find ourselves resembles, in many ways, the pre-Christendom world of the first four centuries after Christ—a world in which the church was not only *not* privileged, but also ridiculed and dismissed by most and persecuted by some. Participation in worship and the life of the worshipping community was counter-cultural and took exceptional effort. The world simply did not make room for it, whether in its structuring of daily life or in social expectations.

The pre-Christendom church, however, was recognized as radical, threatening the status quo. While persecuted, however, it was fearfully admired for its faith and action. Its worship encompassed not only the spiritual, but the whole of life. The Story of God's self-revelation in Jesus Christ was at the center of its communal life. The expectation that God's Spirit was at work in the community was evident as the poor were fed. Often, when contagious disease threatened the population, Christians were the only ones to care for the ill. Without the privileges that it would be granted with the rise of Christendom, Christianity grew rapidly during this period as it responded to its time and situation. The time and situation in which we find ourselves today is similar.

Though the new reality of postmodernism presents great challenges for the church, therefore, it also provides great opportunities for ministry and mission. Some thirty years ago, a noted Mennonite historian researched Anabaptist/Mennonite worship and established that "the Anabaptists sought to be faithful in their generation and interpreted the biblical materials in the context of their time. . . . We in turn must interpret the biblical materials for our time. This means the biblical record has priority. It also means that our historical situation, so different from theirs, will cause us to see the issues differently, and therefore may lead to new interpretations."[11]

The post-Christendom, postmodern world challenges us to re-imagine worship as a full-being experience welcomingly engaging any and all of our senses, an art in its own right, and one in which the arts hold an integral, unique place. Worship, spirituality, and the arts share characteristics that speak boldly and deeply in a postmodern world. Each one "attempts to name mystery, calls us to see in new and fuller ways, is grounded in incarnation, and is a catalyst for conversion."[12]

Living in the Tension

The tension of Christian worship, of Christian life, has always been there. The familiarity and surety that could prevail in the reason-dominated modern era, riding the privilege of Christendom, tended to keep that tension obscured, unaddressed, and largely unacknowledged. Yet this most basic tension of living and working and worshipping in the absence of the tidy supports of Christendom and modernism, as did the early church, is at the heart of doing theology in our postmodern world.

God is love, yet the world is filled with hatred and division. God is community, yet loneliness is epidemic. God is gracious, yet so many in crushing poverty, endemic violence, unrelenting injustice and unpredictable retribution. God is welcoming, yet so many are excluded. God is whole, yet life is filled with brokenness. The mystery and beauty of resurrection is paired inexorably with the ugliness and cruelty of a criminal's cross. We seek to be faithful, yet know ourselves to be unfaithful. And so goes the endless paradox that we face, living in a world in which the kingdom of God is both here and not yet here. These are full-being aches that call for full-being grappling.

Worship that grows out of the tension of such paradox must include gracious spaces:
- opportunities for all gathered for worship to participate in it;
- art that can be handled by eyes and hands, giving the imagination room to roam;
- the stuff of our common life brought to our common worship;
- our willingness to sit with questions and paradox and mystery, acknowledging that revelation will come over time, like the layers of an onion.

To employ the arts integrally in worship is to seek, in the context of our generation, to be faithful in the interpretation of the biblical story.

If theology seeks to understand and reflect critically our faith, and if much that is vital to faith is poetic and imaginative, then a theology incapable of appreciating and interpreting what is poetic and imaginative about faith will have no way of finishing its job.

— *Frank Burch Brown*
  Arts, Theology and the Church:
  New Intersections

Idols and Icons

There may still be some, however, who would raise the question—or express a fear—of idolatry. It is true that any element of worship can be given "idol" status. Idolatry happens when we mistake something for that which it represents, "forgetting that its true function is to point beyond itself."[13] Could our music become idolatrous if the quality of the music becomes more important than the God it praises or more important than the community gathered for worship? Could a tradition of plainness, with its right angles and stark walls, become a point of stiff pride rather than an avenue to praise? Could a tradition of privileging the sermon above all else make an idol of words? An idol may be lurking when any element of worship takes on undue importance—when it cannot be altered in any way without causing controversy, or the when expectations for it become unreasonably high.

Let's consider a different word: *icon*. Today it is increasingly rare to find a four-year-old child who cannot point to the icon on a computer screen, knowing that her favorite program will appear and open with the click of the mouse. The concept of the icon is important because it moves our conversation in the direction of thinking about theology, revelation, and full-being responses in a postmodern world.

The icon didn't come into being, however, with the advent of computers. It is a centuries-old tradition of art that is very different from the western view with which most of us are most familiar. When we go to a museum, we look at a painting by standing back and scanning it for clues. In post-Medieval western art there is usually a point along the horizon line known as the vanishing point, toward which everything recedes. This sense of perspective feels natural to us because it reinforces our sense of how we experience the world around us. This sense of rightness allows us to feel a certain sense of control, perhaps even mastery, as we move on to the next painting.

Icons, on the other hand, turn our sense of perspective on its head. Instead of the vanishing point being out there somewhere, we who view the icon *are* the vanishing point. Instead of standing aloof, in a position of control outside the work, we are addressed by the icon. The icon confronts us and draws us into a mystery that opens ever more deeply before us. Icons are windows of a sort. Their purpose is not to be the object of our gaze, but to point to something beyond.

The art of worship, and the arts that make up the elements of worship, are like icons. They are not God. They do not, cannot, capture the fullness of God. Instead, they invite us, eyes wide open, to look for God. Looking through these windows, we use our God-given imaginations to see something of God. We experience revelation as "ideas are struck together

Visuals are a huge part of helping people enter the story.

— *Pauline Steinmann*
Saskatoon, Saskatchewan

The whole purpose of the visuals is to bring you into God's presence, to help you know that God is in this place.

— *LaVerle Schrag*
Hutchinson, Kansas

and sparks leap through the air between them, revealing familiar notions in a new light."[14] Art created for worship that proclaims the fullness of God in Trinity, and the imprint of the Trinity upon God's people, will be art that calls us into a deeper understanding of the God we praise. It also reflects back to us who we are and whom God calls us to be.

Imagining Worship

Our society is increasingly complex and demanding. The forces competing for our hearts and minds grow stronger, dividing us even as they conspire to homogenize us. Advertisers use to their advantage culturally-created longings, playing to all our senses. Our visual literacy is extremely high. Our postmodern world longs for encounter with the mystery of God and the God of mystery, for a genuine experience of welcome and community, and for a reality beyond the promises of countless infomercials and pop culture's never-ending torrent of words.

In this postmodern world, to honor the work of "turning" into artistic medium what was found in revelation is imperative, not just a question to be considered. Mennonite poet Jean Janzen offers this modest proposal:

> *I propose that the arts could move us into a stronger faith. In a time when much of modern society has lost a sense of the divine, holy space, when our worship tends toward the familiar, feel-good style, we need to hear a new and stringent call to encounters with God that recognizes [God's] immensity and [God's] intimacy. The making and experiencing of art in our lives can be a powerful vehicle to recover what we began to lose during the Reformation, a true sense of awe. I propose that the power of art to reveal truth about God, our time, and ourselves becomes an effective tool for change, the kind of change which is needed for effective kingdom work.*[15]

To see, to hear, to taste, to smell, to touch, to experience, to feel, to know—all of our senses, both physical and internal, can be available to, and primed for, the work of imagination. This work is central to doing theology, encountering revelation, and forming response. Employing all the arts in worship—word, song, visual art, drama, movement, ritual—makes gracious space for the eyes of the imagination, open at their widest. It creates gracious space for God—invisible, indivisible and inexhaustible—to choose rich and varied modes of revelation. It opens gracious space for our God-given creativity to give birth to our responses, and for us to be formed and transformed as we worship together. Come and see. God is here among us and worthy of our praise.

We're just beginning to understand the interplay between vision and worship, imagination and the written word—that it's actually, if you think about it, all one piece.

— *Lynette Wiebe*
  Winnipeg, Manitoba

To find the extraordinary hidden in the ordinary, we are called to participate in God's own imagination—to see ourselves, our neighbors, and our world through God's eyes, full of possibility, full of promise, ready to be transformed.

— *Barbara Brown Taylor*
  The Preaching Life

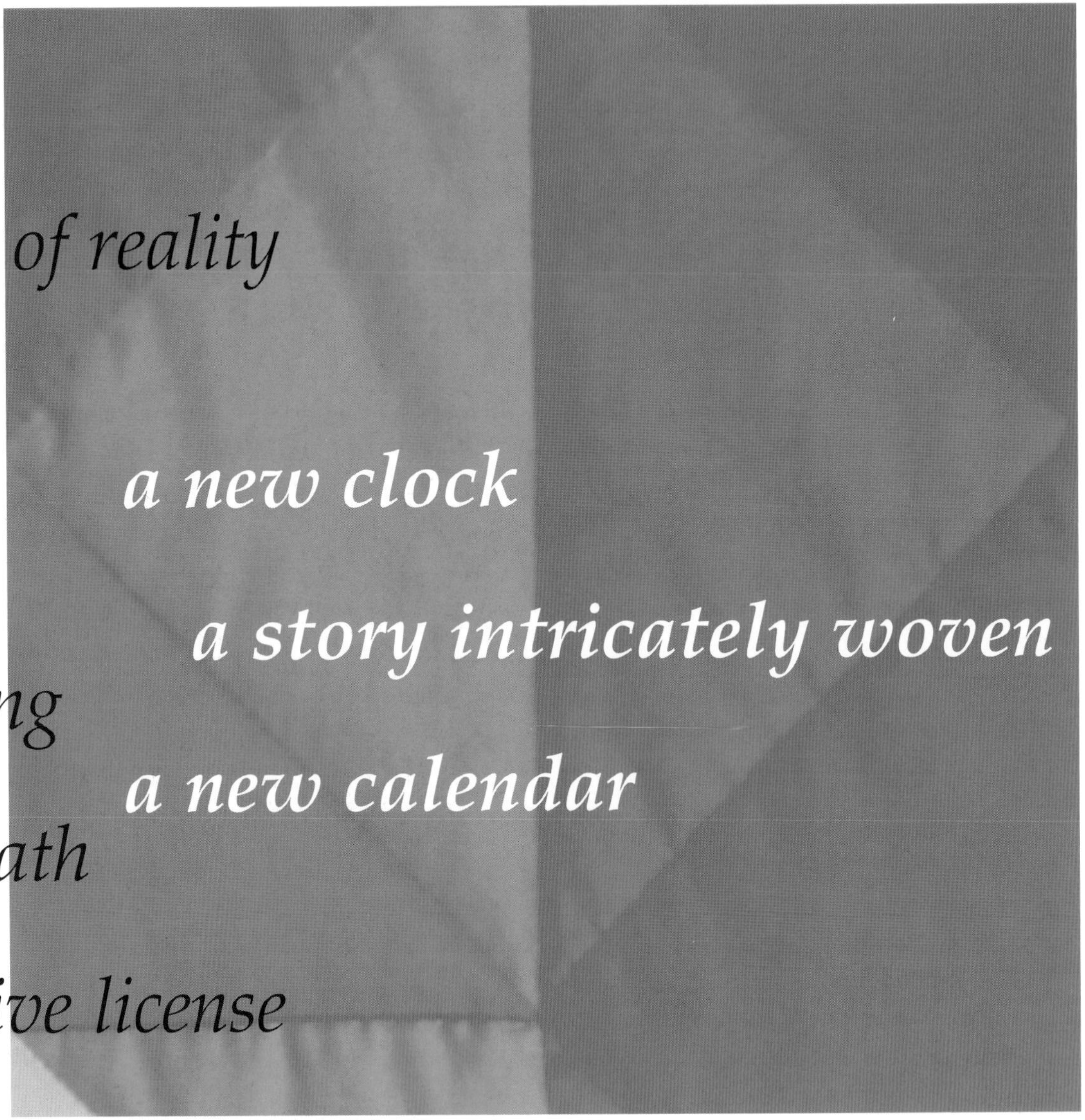

an acknowledgment of reality

an engaging mystery

liturgical freedom

a place of gathering

a new clock

a story intricately woven

a trustworthy ritual path

a new calendar

imaginative license

room and reason to participate

a wordless sanctuary

Chapter 2

The Scripture We Proclaim

What you hear whispered, proclaim from the housetops.
—Matthew 10:27

Come *and see. Listen to me. Take and eat. Reach out your hand. Do this and remember.* Invitations to full-being participation fill the stories of Jesus' life and ministry. God-Among-Us chooses story and illustration drawn from the common stuff of our lives to reveal the very face of the God we praise. With that in mind, let's begin this chapter with a story. Gather in a little closer. Make sure you're where you can see and hear and imagine being with Jesus.

> *One day, people brought their children to Jesus so that he could touch them. When the disciples saw this happening, they sternly ordered the people to stop it. Now when Jesus saw this, it made him angry. He said to the disciples, "Let the little children come to me; don't stop them, because the Kingdom of God belongs to those who come like children. Here's the truth: Those who don't receive the Kingdom of God like a little child will miss it." Then, smiling, he turned to the children gathered close all around him, and he picked them up in his arms and blessed them.*[1]

When children come for a story, they come with a sense of wonder, expecting to enter in. They are ready to feel the hot sun or the cool water on their skin, to draw back when things get scary, or to experience the reassurance of a path safely found. Whenever they hear an invitation to look or taste or touch, they enter the story as ready participants. Children come with their imaginations poised and waiting, eyes wide open, senses primed, and anticipation heightened. They come as full-being participants, and as the story unfolds, they offer full-being responses.

That's exactly how the Scripture invites us to come as worship planners, whether we are

The Bible is full of universal archetypal images that transcend culture and language: bread, shared meals, seeds, lost sons, dying children, aged parents with cloudy eyes, and pain as vivid as a spear thrust into the side of a dying man.

— *Robin R. Meyers*
   With Ears to Hear

preparing sermon or song, visual art or movement. That's exactly how theology is done and revelation happens. Early childhood specialists are quick to remind us that play, using the imagination, is the work of children as they learn about their world, begin to understand relationship, and catch glimpses of who they will one day become. As we approach the task of proclamation, therefore, we hang onto an image of the full-being play that comes naturally to children.

The Scripture we proclaim did not start as neat chronology, completely cross-referenced. It was passed on orally, holding within it the memory of God's interactions with shepherds, prophets, despots, and the nameless. It formed the people of God in its retelling, remembering, and reliving. The Bible we hold today is the weaving together of that narrative of encounters with the God we praise. Underlying our approach to proclamation by design is a fundamental understanding that Scripture is story—the Story of God. Scripture is the Story that reveals the shape of who we become as "people of the Word." Our charge, as worship planners, is to discover what it takes to lift the Story off the page for our community, and then, in remembering and reliving it, to invite them into the Story as full-being participants, wide-eyed and expecting to see God.

The Grand Narrative

A fancier word for *story* is *narrative*. The two words can be used interchangeably, but more often, *narrative* describes an especially important story that tells us how to understand and live our lives. Scripture, the Story of encounters with the God of Trinity, is narrative with many parts. For people of the Word, it is *the* Narrative, *the* defining story for life in all its dimensions. The implications of this story for our lives are immense and complex, too filled with mystery, to ever be exhausted. It's no accident that Jesus chose to draw the grand Narrative together by telling stories.

Story engages us deeply because it provides both distance and immediacy.[2] Remember the story that the prophet Nathan told King David in 2 Samuel 12? Nathan's tale about a rich man taking the poor man's lamb described David's sin, but it was removed enough that David could hear the story, identify the wrong, empathize with the victim, and pronounce fitting justice for the perpetrator. Then, having experienced the story through the characters, David could recognize and acknowledge his own transgression.

Story does not *demand* that we participate. Instead, it creates gracious space and *invites*

us to participate.[3] In a story, we imagine the characters moving about in their circumstances in ways we find difficult to imagine in our own lives. Then, from the distance of story, we can go on to draw parallels, come to self-recognition, discover truths that were not so easily recognized from within our experience. Narrative is how our minds organize both our memories and the dreams we hope to live into.

As we interviewed worship leaders in our denomination, they told and retold one especially powerful story. While the particulars were different in each telling, it became clear that a visual focus used one year in the denominational Lenten worship guide had a deep impact. The guide, entitled "Broken and Blessed" focused on the acknowledgment of our brokenness and God's restorative work in our lives. Worshippers arrived on the first Sunday of Lent to find the jagged fragments of a very large clay vessel gathered on the worship center. Then, throughout the Sundays of Lent, the pot was slowly put back together. On Easter Sunday, restored but not yet perfect, still bearing the scars of its brokenness, it held the flowers that proclaimed Christ's resurrection.

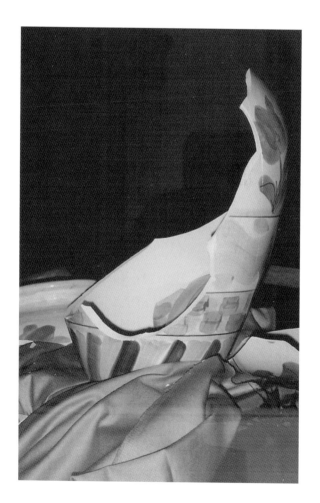

- *The year we did the broken pot . . . we heard more stories from people about their brokenness . . . than I can remember.*
- *I remember people talking about how watching that pot come back together was a sermon in its own right.*
- *Our church was going through a very difficult time of conflict and I know that it was very meaningful.*
- *The brokenness of that really spoke to people about their own brokenness.*

The pot, in all its stages, bore witness to the season's Scripture texts, lifting them off the page and giving life to them. As the Story was retold each week, it mixed with our stories and evoked memories of fragments that needed to be restored to wholeness in our lives. A broken clay vessel spoke eloquently and forcefully; the visual display invited worshippers to draw parallels in their lives, and to allow self-recognition to dawn. Truths waited to be discovered in congregations across the church.

When the writers of the guide first came to these Lenten stories with their imaginations ready and with their senses primed, the revelation they encountered was a common clay pot, broken and in need of restoration and wholeness. This is the work to which all worship planners are called. Admittedly, not every image we encounter, not every retelling we shape, will make such a wide, indelible impression. But when we come to our work with our imaginations at the ready and our eyes wide open, we can be sure that in that playful space, the God of the Scripture we proclaim waits to be revealed.

The Storyteller's Box

It is not unusual for storytellers to have a box or bag or basket out of which they pull objects that will help set the story in context and illustrate it as it unfolds. These things, most often common objects of everyday life, inspire wonder and connection as the hearers look or listen, touch or taste. A storyteller has to enter into the story as a child, with imagination, to discover the right things to pull out of the box at story time.

As worship planners, we have just such a box at our disposal. Like the storyteller's box, it can help us illustrate the ongoing Story of the God we praise. What are some of the things we will find in the box? Let's see, there's . . .

. . . a calendar

Calendars help us keep track of the passage of time. Important dates are often highlighted in red. Many calendars feature photographs each month to remind us of the passage of the seasons. Almost every calendar leaves room for us to write events from our own lives that we need to remember or anticipate. At the end of the year, we look at that calendar and see our story, right there before us.

The church also has a calendar that highlights important dates and seasons. This calendar always invites us to merge our stories with the Story. Known variously as the "Christian Year," the "Church Year" or the "Liturgical Year," this calendar begins with the first Sunday of Advent, a season of waiting for Christ's appearing. Instead of marking national or greeting-card-generated holidays, it marks significant events in the life and ministry of God-Among-Us. It ends with Christ the King Sunday, an occasion to look back across the calendar to realize how, over the year, the Story has been retold, remembered, and relived. This calendar causes us to reflect on ways in which the Story and our story have met and intertwined.

The Christian Year is a radical calendar that reorders our days and our seasons. A season of waiting and preparation gives way to a season of celebration and praise that makes way for a season of service and response. This calendar reorders our faith and our lives by inviting us to embody the Incarnation in its retelling, remembering, and reliving. Round and round—God transforms us in the ongoing turning of the seasons.

It's a tension and a paradox. You need to pay attention to the details and it's something so far beyond you, but somewhere in that tension is where we make worship and find God . . . It fits into the mystery of how and where we meet God . . . What you realize is—people are working out theology through those things.

— *Deb Schmidt*
Hutchinson, Kansas

. . . a clock

Whereas a calendar sets the rhythm of the year, a clock helps us pay attention to the particulars. Time passes, and the Christ candle is lit, signaling the transition from the waiting of Advent to the celebration of Christmas. Time passes, signaled by a change of color in the worship space. "Where are the plants, the banners, the color?" we ask. And then it sinks in—it's Lent. A few months later, the greens of Ordinary Time signal open, inviting space for response, exploration, and service. Time passes, and each week we are called to a Sabbath space of rest and renewal.

Round and round. Our clock is radical in its ordering of our time. When we enter as full-being participants, worship has its own sense of time. "Lost in wonder, love and praise," we cease to be aware of our watches, and the time is "neither long nor short, but simply lasts until it is finished"[4]—a space known as liminal time. Our clock radically calls us to live our lives out of a sense of seamless, eternal time, rather than being caught up in the menacing, unrelenting time of the culture around us.

See "The Liturgical Year" and "The Colors of the Liturgical Year" on pages 89 and 91.

. . . sign, symbol, sacrament, and ritual

Things to see and hear, things to touch and taste, common things from our common life, things from the box that invite us to full-being participation and full-being response—that's what we are talking about when we refer to signs, symbols, sacraments, and ritual. In many a free-church or "non-liturgical" congregation, these have long been uncomfortable words. They need not be. Mennonite theologian and historian, John Rempel offers some brief definitions and examples that may help us think more clearly about them:

- A sign designates the reality to which it points in a way that makes common sense (e.g., smoke as a sign of fire).
- A symbol is an object that evokes cosmic or historical realities that cannot be reduced to a single word or object (e.g., the cross is a symbol of the Gospel to those initiated into its meaning).
- A sacrament [in Christian terms] is a repeated action initiated by Jesus and bearing the promise of his presence (e.g., the Lord's Supper).
- A ritual is the totality of words and gestures that brings a symbol or sacrament to life.[5]

Part of being human is to use the common objects and actions of our lives to give meaning to things. It is our way of giving voice and form to that for which words alone are inadequate. Jesus spoke of living water, sought out baptism, and washed his disciples' feet. He spoke of grains of wheat, fed thousands, and took bread and broke it. We cannot recall these words or actions without stories coming to mind from Scripture—and from our experience. When we see a chalice, a basin and towel, or a pitcher on Sunday morning, we need not look at our bulletin to know what the service will hold. A whole world of meaning and memory, hopes and dreams, opens in front of us before a word is said or a song is sung. We gather around a table, serving one another, or we meet the eyes of one standing near us as we "pass the peace," and we recognize ourselves as the body of Christ. John Rempel shares this story of recognition:

> *The most memorable part of the day of my initiation into the Ottawa Street Men- nonite Brethren church was not baptism itself but the communion service that concluded it. A solemnity descended on the congregation that told me more was happening here than met the eye; when I looked into the cup I knew we were in the presence of a greater reality than we had words for. I had experienced the mystery of grace; I had "touched and handled things unseen."*[6]

Such signs and symbols, sacrcaments and rituals, are at the heart of our communal life together. What we do together shapes the people we become together. It is through these that we can see and hear, touch and taste, move and respond. The use of symbols and symbolic actions recognizes "that we cannot enter the mystery of God and experience the healing, transforming love of God if we do not begin with our senses."[7] Through them we practice the "not yet" in the imperfect "already." Through them, over time and in community, we are transformed.

Calendar, clock, sign, symbol, sacrament, and ritual are in our storyteller's box. They help us put God's Story—and our stories—in context, and they help us illustrate the ongoing unfolding of these stories in the life of the congregation. They are familiar, and they are powerful. They hold deep meaning, and they invite new understandings. They ground us, even as they call us to transcendence. Through them we are established, even as we are transformed. Like the storyteller, our task as worship planners is to enter into the Story with our imaginations and to discover how our box can invite our particular congregations into the Story as full-being participants.

See "Planning Pearls," page 99.

Midrash

In the previous chapter we used the familiar yet ancient concept of the icon to describe the way in which the art and arts of worship serve as windows through which we are invited to see something of God. Let's consider another ancient concept to talk about the work of interpreting Scripture, of lifting the texts off the page and bringing them into the worshipping assembly. The *midrash* comes out of the centuries-old Jewish experience of grappling with Scripture. The Hebrew word means "to seek out" or "to inquire."[8] Midrash is what Jesus did when he told stories from the Old Testament and then broke them open in the lives of those gathered around him.

The tradition of midrash holds the use of God-given imagination at its core. It seeks to break open the Scripture in new ways that are accessible in a contemporary setting. While many techniques of interpretation may be employed, "all are characterized by a profound respect for the text itself and a remarkable freedom to extend and elaborate on the text."[9]

We introduce midrash here because it honors the work of imagination. This ancient practice, interestingly, shows itself to be quite postmodern. Midrash honors the silences in Scripture, recognizing that what is not said may be as significant as what is said. It leaves gracious spaces for us to use our imagination in a variety of media. In the process it holds together two practices that have often been separated in a reason-dominated, process-oriented world: exegesis and hermeneutics. Ask anyone who has been to seminary and their eyes will roll as they recall these two processes they were carefully taught to follow. Exegesis is the process of getting at what the text *meant* to the original audience. Hermeneutics is about getting to what the text *means* in this time and place. We do midrash when we hold the two together, honoring the text and inviting the imagination to lead us to new discoveries.

Lest we become overwhelmed with this responsibility of taking that which we have heard, seen, felt, and sensed in Scripture and presenting it afresh—we do well to harken back to our earlier discussion of theological imagination and to Walter Klaassen's charge to continue to "interpret the biblical materials for our time."[10] This ongoing task of interpretation falls not just to those charged with worship planning. As the *Confession of Faith in a Mennonite Perspective* reminds us, the "insights and understandings which we bring to the interpretation of the Scripture are to be tested in the faith community."[11] As worship planners, we merely begin the conversation with our midrash and provide gracious space for the conversation to continue. "It's what we call the hermeneutic community; we're drawn together, we interpret together, we live together. We don't just sit in the presence of the Word; we sit with

Sacraments not only hallow the stuff of the world; they also hallow our handling of that stuff. They give us something to look at, something to taste and smell, something to feel upon our skin and experience for ourselves. They give us something to do with our hands and with our bodies as well— The experience of them exceeds our understanding of them. Reaching out to handle God, it is we who are handled, gently but with powerful effect.

—*Barbara Brown Taylor*
  The Preaching Life

Our work is not so much to make the holy visible as it is to proclaim the holy is present.

—*Nancy Chinn*
  Spaces for Spirit

various interpretations, making meaning together."[12] Come closer. Gather round. Enter the story. Become part of the conversation.

Doing Midrash

As worship planners, our work is midrash. We lift the Scripture we proclaim off the page, discovering ways in which we will invite our communities into the Story as full-being participants, wide-eyed and expecting to see God. And how is it, again, that we are invited to come to the story? Like children—ready to participate, ready to engage in the work of children: to exercise our imaginations, with senses primed and anticipation heightened.

Where do we begin? The symbol used for this chapter is the square, calling to mind the shape of the Bible we hold. This four-square shape, with its equal sides and 90-degree angles, might suggest a predictable, prescribed pattern of approach to our work—start here, move from left to right, from top to bottom and back again. But the Bible we hold is simply the container for the stories of encounters with God, woven back and forth through peoples and events, time and eternity. Within its covers are recitations of history, bits of poetry, portraits drawn, interactions reported, teachings to be remembered, and even ledger-like accountings. Together, they form the Story and the roots of our faith. Roots most often take less regular paths, weaving around and through the rich soil rather than following the shape of the container that holds both soil and roots.

So it is with the work of midrash. You won't find a prescriptive sequence endorsed here. Those who love steps and formulas may be disappointed at first. Following the roots, echoing the journey of the cyclical Christian calendar, the turn of time, the rotation of worship leaders, and the round-trip between Jerusalem and Emmaus—the artistic process, too, meanders. Imaginations at the ready, we discover entry into this gently turning, faithful creativity. As our interviewees told us, we might . . .

. . . begin with a medium
"I'm waiting to do something that includes the ceiling of the entire space," an artist says. "I'm not quite sure what it is yet, but I think when the time is right, we'll know it." The artist has a design, but is waiting for revelation. *Waiting* is a fitting description of the posture of many worship artists. In that place of disciplined eagerness, preachers can gestate a sermon idea for hours on end. In a month permeated with snowy red bows, a quilter stitches purple

Scripture was first put into our hands not as *prescription* for life but as a *description* of it, full of wisdom intended to serve us in our living of it.

—*Barbara Brown Taylor*
The Preaching Life

thread into a Lenten banner in order to be ready. A dancer practices a symbolic flourish until it becomes second nature to her body. This "second nature" will free the congregation of awkward distraction, enabling them to see the symbol for what it is. This takes time. A choir rehearses an anthem weeks before the Spirit reveals the right Sunday to sing it. Waiting in one's preferred medium is one place to begin. *What designs are the artists in your congregation thinking about?*

... begin with material

"My eyes are always open for things that will work for something at some point," says one worship planner. His files are marked *light, water, earth,* and *bread*. "Rarely is anything just an object to me . . . I'm always looking for symbols of faith." Materials, ready and waiting, are discovered as the things that will help lift the Story off the page—including large, empty picture frames that others might have seen no earthly reason to keep. "I had a great time at the fabric store . . ." says another artist. Pieces of sycamore bark become a mobile, turning and cascading gently during a season of leave-taking. Materials, stored away, waiting for the right time, can invite entry into the Story in new and profound ways. *What materials might be waiting to become storytellers in your congregation?*

... begin with revelation

"It all needs to be about bringing us into God's presence and helping us be aware of God. If any of these designs do that without being the focal point themselves, then I think they have a place in worship." Here we have not only a starting point in theology, but also criteria for evaluation. If the art halts the eye at its own appearance, if the art does anything but provide gracious space and invite worship, it needs to go. An awareness of God, unseen but everywhere visible, is a good place to begin—and to end. *What is the fundamental awareness of God in your congregation?*

... begin with the imagined community

"How do I help people think about the Ten Lepers and what it meant for the one returning to be a Samaritan? How do I help the congregation think about what that meant at that time?" Here the design is influenced by pastoral care—by a desire to help a gathered body envision an insight that resonates meaningfully in the mind of the one proclaiming. Though the artist, in this instance, is describing the composition of a sermon, she adds, "Sometimes the images come to me that convey the thing before all the words come to me. It's not like I

The artist always starts with something in the world—objects, colors, shapes—and collects and draws out the "sense" that the Creator has placed in these things, and shapes this into an image of meaning.

—William A. Dyrness
Visual Faith

do the sermon and then try to find something to fit." *How will our congregation best see and hear this important message?*

. . . begin with denominational materials

"I wait for inspiration. *(Hearty chuckle.)* Well, obviously with Lent and Advent I start with the worship materials and that triggers some thinking and we go from there." Many denominations provide worship resources for the major seasons of the church year. Their visual and ritual suggestions need critical adaptation and artistic discernment, taking into account the community in which they are used. A congregation on the Saskatchewan prairies adapts Advent materials to reflect their experience of the Northern Lights breaking into the darkness of mid-winter. A community on the plains of Kansas reflects the starkness and repentance of Lent with tree branches downed in a devastating ice storm. An assembly in Florida adapts a rented space with three arches that form a frame to highlight the creek, lush foliage, and abundant sunlight that streams through their windows. The adaptations are local and communal. *How effective is this material in communicating to our congregation?*

. . . begin with what already exists

Upon reading a text together, a worship committee looks at one another, asking excitedly and almost in unison, "What about that sculpture?" Another group notices that their congregation's logo, with branches reaching high and roots extending deep, seems to have been created with the Scripture story in mind. "Does anyone remember that Rembrandt painting of the prodigal son?" asks someone from a different planning group. Existing designs are thus found to be apt for proclamation, and are offered in service to the gospel for a particular Sunday or season. *What images are already available out there or in our experience, that will break the Story open?*

. . . begin with Scripture

"The text runs through my mind the entire time I'm working on the design. Scripture has to be an integral part of the visual even when it's not there physically to read. Having it run through my mind keeps the visual true." The text comes to life and then the visual takes on a life. When the congregation exclaims together, "Oh! That's how this is speaking!" we know that the artists have made effective design choices to transfer the image of one planner or preacher or artist or committee to the prayers of the assembly. *In your congregation, how will your encounters with God in Scripture become invitations to receive revelation?*

This is certainly not meant to be an exhaustive list. What matters is not a prescriptive creative sequence, some step-by-step process. The disciplines of proclamation are primarily two: awareness of the holy (expecting to see God) and awareness of which expression best fits with the other assembled words, actions, and people. "We live in a world that invariably reflects God's values and even features echoes of God's presence," writes William A. Dyrness. "Artists, by virtue of their special gifts and sensitivities, are uniquely able to capture and reflect these values in their work."[13] The artists we spoke to were often silent for some time before answering our query about beginning. When they spoke, here are some of the things we heard:

- *Scripture is where I start . . . ahead of time . . . to make connections with other things around me . . . pay attention to what colors or images come up.*
- *I look at the text . . . then it's all of your life that comes into play . . . things you've seen . . . experiences you've had.*
- *There are times when part of the process grabs me, surprises me, and pulls me in . . .*
- *Reading the text . . . letting it sink in . . . just living with it for awhile.*
- *A process of percolation . . .*
- *The very first step is prayer, prayer that gets God acquainted with the current project. Ideas come from . . . things I see or think about, from reading and research, other people, deep inside me, from listening to God.*
- *As for process, I turn to* Transparent Confession. *There is an energy and blessing in laying hold of the materials at hand and letting an expression emerge.*
- *When the banner was hung in the sanctuary I had a profound feeling of finishedness. I really felt it was no longer mine . . . I felt fulfilled just by having done what I felt God was doing and I didn't need anything else.*

Invitation to Wonder

Not only is there no step-by-step sequence that must be followed as we do midrash, sometimes there are multiple points of entry at work simultaneously. And sometimes, even though we have our imaginations at the ready and our anticipation heightened, those multiple points of entry come together as surprising and profound revelations of the God we praise. Here's just such a story:

Scripture sometimes reports satisfying, full-scale divine theophanies, like fire from heaven that consumed the water drenched altar on Mt Carmel, with the priests of Baal looking on in horrified amazement. More often, however, God chooses to work on the human scale, in the ordinary ebb and flow of life.

—*Leanne Van Dyk*
A More Profound Alleluia

[The Bible is] a conversation partner . . . searching for the point of contact, something that will quicken the imagination and prompt a conversation worth having and worth hearing.

—*Robin R. Meyers*
With Ears to Hear

Because worship is the primary setting in which the congregation is corporately formed in faith, the fullest possible understanding of God needs to be expressed and experienced in that context.

— Marlene Kropf
Elkhart, Indiana

As the first anniversary of 9/11, 2001, approached, the Hope Mennonite community felt a deep need to mark the anniversary in some significant way. There was a strong desire to acknowledge the feelings of loss, vulnerability, fear, and anger that had become part of the fabric of life, and to pray for healing in the face of such brokenness.

Esther Kreider Eash, a member of the congregation, was in her New York office on the morning of September 11th and, in the days that followed, shared the experience of chaos and coping in the city. When the decision was made to hold the service of remembrance, Esther, an artist, was invited to create the worship center. While others helped her carry in several loads of broken concrete, bricks and tiles and jagged pieces of metal and wire, Esther was left alone to work with her carefully chosen materials.

On Sunday morning the congregation gathered in a darkened worship space. Standing alone at the center of the platform was the dimly spotlighted worship center covered with rubble, unrelenting, except for two thin green shoots and the glow of the Christ candle rising from within a broken water tile. Not visible were a number of small dishes of oil. The service was planned in a rhythm of reading, confession, singing and silence, beginning with angry lament from the Psalms and moving toward prayers for healing. The worship center remained the sole visual focus until the pastor stepped onto the platform and invited the congregation's shepherds forward to take a dish of oil and then invited the assembly to come for anointing.

When the service ended, many sat quietly and continued to focus on the worship center, where the dishes of anointing oil were now set prominently atop the piles of rubble. Others approached the worship center, studying, touching, lingering. The image of remembrance and hope created for that morning became an important experience of community and healing in the congregation. Esther reflects that themes of rebirth, forgiveness, and hope came together as she worked: "It was like, 'Okay, I've come full circle. I'm ready to move forward.' For me, it was a surprise. I didn't even know that I was thinking things through that needed to be thought through."[14]

This is what an invitation to full-being participation looks like. Gracious space for interpretation, revelation, and full-being response. Senses engaged. Stories of lament and hurt, presence and healing, lifted off the page and proclaimed as the various arts of worship bring together the Story and our story. Not always will we begin with theological discourse. Not every art piece will begin with formal exegesis—though, given its function in Christian worship, Scripture acts as guiding source. We must resist the temptation to attempt to shape the community in any particular way, however desirable the outcomes of mission, morality, and maturity may be. While these outcomes may occur, proclamation is simply the art of bringing the Story forward to mix with our story and inviting the gathered assembly to participate, converse, and respond. In the gracious space created there, the God we proclaim awaits those who come.

Continuing the Conversation

Our role as worship planners is twofold. We come to the story first, find what waits in the box to help the Story come off the page, and, with imaginations fired up, discover revelation of the God we praise. Then, through the arts of worship, we interpret that revelation in ways that invite the community into the Story. That's where the first role ends. Then we are invited to re-enter the Story a second time on Sunday morning and experience it anew—like children—with the worshippers who gather. It may well be that the art we created and installed is not yet done with us.

On the potter's wheel of corporate worship, private devotion, and the study of Scripture, the church rotates in time, kept soft by prayer. Those who artfully proclaim the gospel subject themselves, personally, to its shaping influence. New insight may occur at any turn, the hands of God continually remaking creation. "Thy will be done," we pray, and we become wet clay once more. Potters call this "open time," the time available to have one's way with malleable material. Engagement with biblical imagery in word, ritual, or visual art is one of the church's open times. We, too, are invited to come, eyes wide open, expecting to see God.

The invitation is simple and compelling. We come with a sense of wonder, expecting to enter in, to feel the hot sun and the cool water on our skin, to draw back when things get scary, and to experience the reassurance of a path safely found. We enter in as ready participants when we hear the invitation to look or taste or touch. We come with our imaginations at the ready, our senses primed, and our anticipation heightened. We come to the Story—the Scripture we proclaim—as children. In that playful space we will encounter the God we praise. As our stories mix with the Story, we comprehend more about relationships with God in Trinity, with one another, and with those all around us. We catch glimpses of who it is that we will become as we live out of and into the Story. It seems only natural that what we hear whispered we cannot help but proclaim from the rooftops.

The history of Christian faith and theology is also a history of the eyes, the ears, of bodily gestures and movement, the mind imagining and the senses conjoining. Wherever human beings hear and encounter the divine, the consequences are poetic, visionary, metaphoric, parabolic, and ordered sound—voices, instruments, and dance.

—*Don E. Saliers*
Arts, Theology, and the Church

Visual art proclaims the good news of the kingdom of God with strong basic design and expressive materials that invite viewer interpretation, encourage interaction, and proclaim the presence of God.

—*Barbara Peterson*
Bristol, Indiana

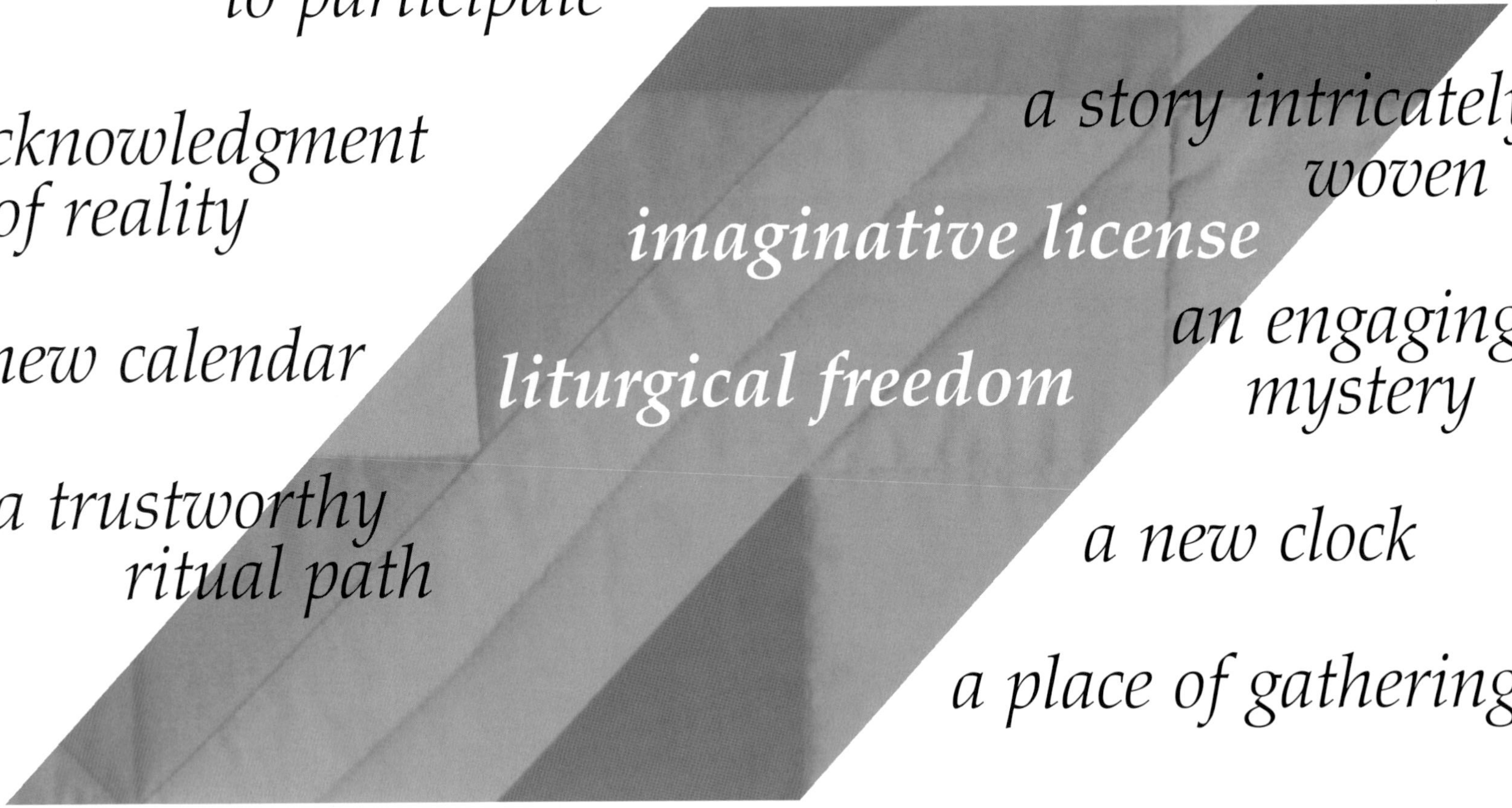

room and reason
to participate

a wordless sanctuary

an acknowledgment
of reality

a story intricately
woven

imaginative license

a new calendar

liturgical freedom

an engaging
mystery

a trustworthy
ritual path

a new clock

a place of gathering

Chapter 3

The Design We Offer

The heavens are telling the glory of God.—Psalm 19:1

Proclamation is the result of our seeing God and our inability to keep such sightings to ourselves. Proclamation *by design* is that union of revelation and expression, that careful selection of expression that best conveys what God has made known. Proclamation *by design* takes biblical images of God's life in the created world and in the kingdom and shares them through the art and arts of worship in the gathered community. Much like creation itself, when we are aroused by an appearance of God's character or activity or purpose, we cannot help but shout from the rooftops.

Psalm 19 exudes proclamation by design. The text reminds us that this design needs no *speech*, or even *words*, not even felt letters on a burlap banner. And though we have excellent acoustics, *their voice is not heard; and yet their voice goes out through all the earth.* Wow! What kind of words are these? Sometimes, the volume comes from high color, resonating symbol and amplified story. Before our very eyes, worship turns to evangelism. Is this not the desire of the gospel? This chapter is a practical discussion on the impractical art of translating meaningful encounters with God into the most meaningful visual expressions of God's unrelenting love and glory.

I think what the abstract has to offer is imagination . . . what the Psalms, the poetry of the Psalms, and the songs we sing, have to offer is that element of imagination. If it's missing from our worship, then we're just going through the motions. We're not being awakened or enlivened. They can awaken the imagination, the possibilities of seeing new things.

—*Joanna Pinkerton*
Wichita, Kansas

Biblical Proclamation by Design

The Psalms are but one of many biblical examples of visual proclamation—images of God proclaimed in the material of earth and flesh. Creation is a design that literally proclaims God's communal nature as Trinity. The church is that design continued, the communal body of Jesus Christ. In the desire for relationship, God establishes covenant with Israel and, though grace is invisible, its symbols and stories most definitely are not. Grace is as perceptible as clouds and pillars, burning shrubs and parted seas, fallen manna, fallen giants, and conception at ninety years of age. Whether in the Old or New Testament, or in the newest

testament of our own lives, covenant is the design that testifies to God's grace.

One Lent, our denominational worship materials invited congregations to compile a scrapbook depicting both the biblical Story of God's love and parallel contemporary stories. The book revealed the profound visibility of "the pursuit of love." Congregations across Canada and the U.S. participated with ease and deep appreciation. Nearly text-free, these scrapbooks told the Story in visible expressions ranging from literal photographs to abstract art, figures of love, visual narratives, metaphors of love, and our most cherished biblical symbols.

The Lenten scrapbooks, like the season, end with images of Jesus' triumph over death, which culminates a long saga of grace and covenant. Earlier, God shapes a design whose very name forecasts its visibility: Emmanuel, God-with-us. Jesus, God Incarnate, *is* the preeminent theological design, the ultimate union of revelation and material expression. The incarnational pattern continues in Jesus' storytelling where his own revelation is regularly paired with fitting expressions of material, symbol and image. Incarnational art and Scripture-shaped worship share in a desire to be seen and handled, claimed and cherished, by the community in whose presence they appear. When symbolic words and wordless symbols join purposes to proclaim God's Word, people are transformed into the holiness they've bathed in, the sacrifice they've swallowed, the justice they've kneaded, the peace they've passed, and the unity they've sung in four strong parts. This, most simply, is the power of a symbol to shape a people.

Hearts and souls come bound together with a story, a vision, a dream, a memory. When we can unite mind and heart, we can form an incarnational truth, God among us, that is life-saving.

— *Nancy Chinn*
  Spaces for Spirit

The Parallelogram of Design

As the triangle was used as a symbol for theology in Chapter 1 and the square to represent Scripture in Chapter 2, this chapter's working template is the parallelogram. It illustrates how art and the arts of worship might be used in the design of worship. One angular side represents the *revelation* and *interpretation* of some aspect of God's character. Revelation comes through careful study, devotional practices, and good pastoral listening, the Monday to Saturday work of preachers and worship leaders. This is theological work and its starting point is the question, "What face of God is revealed in this text?"[1]

Interpretation must then follow. Anabaptists, along with other Protestant Christians, turn primarily to the written Word, devoted to the "task of interpreting the Bible and discerning what God is saying in our time by examining all things in the light of Scripture."[2] Interpretation is a grand treasure hunt, a search for one of Scripture's multifaceted gems. Good worship design carefully decides which facet to accentuate and then lifts it up for God's people gathered in prayer. The artist's own identity seems to vanish as the transparency of both the art and the artist allows meaning to flow into and out of the congregation. Such a presentation decreases distraction and fixes attention upon the One who alone is worthy of our worship.

Medium, the second angled side of the parallelogram, is concerned with the forms that will undergird our praise of God as we gather for worship. Although there are many facets of story and doctrine, truth, and beauty, well-focused worship disciplines itself to a single collaborative design for the duration of the service. It is a discipline preachers readily understand, since not every image that appears during study will appear in the sermon. In the pastoral selection of components, the visual, musical, and verbal focus the light source (revelation plus interpretation), allowing a newly illumined text to rake across the pew. The resulting worship experience is much like turning a diamond.

Modern worship has its own palette: music and prayer, space and time, and the favored medium of Protestant proclamation, preaching. Mennonites have long favored hymn singing as their preferred art form. Now, along with many other denominations, they are also re-discovering the value of worshipping eyes. Alongside the well-crafted sermon and tightly knit doxology, many are finding a dramatic Scripture reading, a Native North American dance, a bouquet of lilies, or a red batik. In one Mennonite church, the pastor recognized the many forms that proclamation had taken one Sunday morning and assumed his position in the pulpit with this happy introit: "Well, we will now hear our third sermon of the morning."[3]

Revelation/interpretation and the *mediums* for our praise are the angled sides of the parallelogram that connect the shape's horizontal lines of *Scripture* and the *worship* we offer as a people. Scripture is constant—the definitive referent to which all worship planning belongs. The corresponding referent is the people's earnest offering of worship, which is as embodied, textured, and colorful as faith itself. Art for worship begins in the mindfulness of faith and the anticipated celebration of the Word. The destination of that art is the participating body that comes expecting the designs of preaching, singing, and prayer to cohere with biblical belief.

Effective proclamation, visual or otherwise, involves finding the best way to describe to the community that which has been revealed in preparations for worship. When this interpretation is brought together with the best sentences, the best songs, the best prayers, and the best images and then offered to the congregation, we have something that *fits*. "Best," how-

Worship planners and leaders today are called to excellence: to keep worship Christ-centered, to call the community to genuine engagement with one another, and to strengthen the links between worship and our life of peace and justice in the world.

—*Marlene Kropf*
Elkhart, Indiana

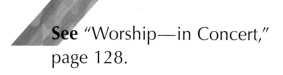

See "Worship—in Concert," page 128.

See "Worship—in Concert," page 128.

It moves . . . it sings . . . it changes and affects the atmosphere of the whole environment.

—*Esther Kreider Eash*
Wichita, Kansas

The visual helps us to see anew
or see things that we haven't seen
before or understand things
in a new way that we haven't
understood before.

— Pauline Steinmann
Saskatoon, Saskatchewan

See "In the Liturgical
Closet," and "Cleaning the
Closet" pages 86 and 115.

ever, has almost nothing to do with professional results and artistic excellence, but everything to do with appropriateness. When it all fits together we have proclamation by design, the parallelogram of God made known. The shape is complete.

Of course, with or without our creative participation, God remains in the business of redemption and true to God's trajectory toward wholeness. All on its own, creation will capably continue testifying to this Good News. When the church chooses to participate creatively, it joins a proclamation already and forever visible in creation. As Psalm 19 shows, creation uses a rich palette of media: moisture, light, pressure, orbit, gravity, and rhythm. Heaven's awareness includes God's glory and everything glorious the sky has to offer.

Installation

Installation can refer to the practical and physical act of placing art in the worship space. It can also refer to the significance of art in the worship life of the assembly.

> *We talk about installing art, but visuals also install something important in our memory, particularly when we use the same images over and over. We have this one favored bridge-type candle holder that comes to mind. When the bridge candle is used, people say, "Oh, that's Jesus. Jesus will be a bridge today between this thing and that thing." We no longer need to process it or explain it because it has become a ritual part of our worship space. Worship will reveal what's being bridged.* [4]

When visual proclamation occurs in worship, it acknowledges that art is not only installed in a church, it is also installed in the church's worship memory, a bridge between liturgical seasons of confession and assurance and service. Just as the firmaments and hours joined the heavens, so the media of words, melody, and visual art conspire to install some aspect of God's glory in the assembly. Worship's parts are always incomplete until they are collaged together and fingered by the people. This joining is called *liturgical installation.* It tells us, first, that worship welcomes human handling, and second, that when worship's thin plies are laminated together into a whole, they help us interpret what we are seeing. *Liturgy* means people must handle it; *installation* means the worship supports it.

In worship, the very pews upon which we sit present an image of worshippers sitting together, thus reminding us to view Scripture's images communally. We are never alone before Scripture. The gospel wants what art wants—to be seen and handled, to evoke wonder, and to inspire response. The interpretive tools we need appear not in felt letters, not even in the bulletin. Time and again, the Mennonite artists we interviewed told us that all the interpretive tools we need lie in the hymns we sing with our eyes open as well as in the prayers we pray as our imagination projects images on our closed eyelids. This is worship installation done well.

Liturgical installation is the essential engagement of the worshipping church. It is the product of worship leaders' work—the elements that beguile, summon, and rouse the church. All of this happens in whatever way God chooses, since worship leaders are merely vessels in God's work, not ring leaders or manipulators. The elements work in concert to create the whole, so that no one element of the service bears the whole of the interpretive burden.

> *Of the five boxes draped in green, littered with tea lights and one big white candle, that big white candle might have, upon entry, been the only recognizable thing on the communion table. It's the Christ Candle. Having sat with it three Sundays into Eastertide, it was a good, familiar place to begin. Then, as worship drew us in, its purpose there on the table began to unfold in its new seasonal context. We began in praise, "Good Shepherd, may I sing thy praise within thy house forever." We confessed our dangerous wandering and prayed, "God of guidance, give us direction so we may know which way to choose and which to refuse." Eventually, John 10 was read, in which Jesus says, "I know my own and my own know me. I am the Good Shepherd." Ah ha! This was Good Shepherd Sunday. After the service, a teary woman approached the pastor with a request for one of the tea lights. "Would it be alright if I took a sheep home with me?" she asked. "That's me. Right there on the edge of that cliff."[5]*

Installed in a supportive liturgy of prayer, Scripture, and song, the symbol took the place of the object, the abstract for the literal. The woman didn't ask for a candle but for "a sheep." This is liturgical installation done well; word and imagery paired for theological precision and the attentive, worshipping community as art's destination.

A misconception that "somehow the sheer weight of the Gospel guarantees its own hearing,"[vi] is what some have called deadly Christian fiction. It is true that the effect of the Word of salvation, liberation, and communion lies beyond our ability and our charge; it is ultimately God's responsibility. But effective communication of that Story is every bit a human task, as essential to worship as it is to mission and Christian education. "The fact is we need to hear that text engaged, amplified, and turned loose in a new form."[7] This is the

When symbols are used well, they allow us to experience a human truth that is a small component of a much greater divine truth.

—Pam Driedger
Altona, Manitoba

playfully serious work of worship planners. How does the visual artist, in cooperation with the rest of the worship planners, proceed?

See "The Evaluation" page 125.

I see myself as being responsible to the community, so I may have something to tell you that will shake you up, but it's still my duty to be in community and serve you with my art.

— *Chuck Regier*
Newton, Kansas

Liturgical Installation

The liturgical artist selects symbols, just as the psalmist did, "according to the logical rightness and necessity of expression, and arranges them within the canons of the artistic medium"[8] in order to express our most fundamental beliefs about God. This advice from a preaching manual describes the medium of words. Because sermons share company in the gallery of all liturgical design, however, the principles can be applied more broadly. When the visual artist is one among several preparing to proclaim the same gospel, and when selections of media are guided by the "logical rightness," we have the beginning of effective liturgy.

But, even with honed intuition, "logical rightness" in collaborative worship planning is a critical skill that many visual artists crave, yet find few resources to develop. "It strikes me that our hymnal is codified, but visually, we fly by the seat of our pants," one artist told us. "Art is like, 'Oh, maybe we should put something visual up, too.' Music is a given. Mennonites know they're going to sing."[9]

By "codified" this artist refers to the system of artistic organization that has long been available to music leaders. In many hymnals, beneath each hymn title are cryptic notations in tiny print, words like Hyfrydol 87.87D. This code refers to the tune title and metrical index. It lets us know that we are singing "Come, thou long-expected Jesus." When two poetic hymn texts correspond metrically, the words can be set to various tunes, their syllables matching notes measure by measure. Such pairings are the result of musical proclamation by intentional design, the fitting union of text and score.

Why do these codified options matter? They matter pastorally because the same melody that we hear in the season of Advent can be used at the time of offering with the words *God, whose giving knows no ending* or sung at a wedding as a blessing. It matters pastorally because one can choose a hearty Russian Kyrie that rejoices in God's mercy or a contemplative Kyrie from France that pleads for God's grace between stanzas of spoken prayer. When the text is what we want and the melody is what we need, we can make choices that result in a mutually enhancing worship design. It just fits. It fits the season, the occasion, the context, the people, and the faith.

This fit is the result of critical decision making and a mark of corporate pastoral care in the disciplined service to a text or idea. Possessed by devotion to interpretation as well as to congregational need, visual artists are asking for the same kind of guiding criteria in their selection of design as musical artists have. This, we heard in our interviews, is church artists' great need. What codes will help them pair the canons of word and artistic medium? What will help them in this work? Who will guide the way?

Something helpful occurs in the conversation between two or more different art forms. Put a musician, a quilter, a cook, and a carpenter in the same room and they will surely find each other and speak something of a common tongue. Suddenly cadence and calico, turmeric and tung oil have sister meanings. Helpful parallels can be drawn between the shape, texture, color, and rhythm of music and those same features in visual art. The familiar language of one art form translated for use in the foreign land of another is a worthy bridge in the gaps of understanding. One artist, speaking of Lenten and Easter banners, referred to them as the "prelude" and "reprise."[10] This is bridging vocabulary we instinctively understand.

At the same time, however, visual proclamation will still require its own criteria for composition, interpretation, evaluation, and liturgical use. In this way, imagery is not mere accessory or pleasant diversion to the sermon. It is an equal partner in the quest to place God's malleable people into God's shaping hands. Whereas preaching helps us hear what forgiveness *sounds* like, art helps us see what reconciliation *looks* like. The "visible Word," writes Karen Stone, is a "companion to the verbal, prophetic, and pastoral Word."[11] Helpful parallels exist, therefore, between formal elements of visual art and other worship activities. This gets us closer to the practicalities of design and installation. But before we explore the practicalities, we must review the purposes of what we are doing in design.

Interpretation

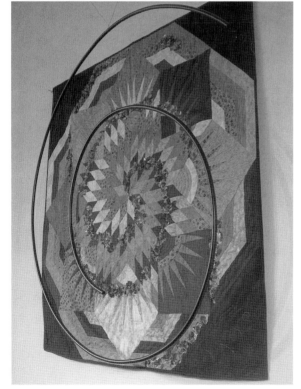

The apprehension that often accompanies artistic engagement stems less from visual illiteracy than from liturgical or theological illiteracy—the failure to understand worship's particular functions and features. Long before we can describe how visual art functions in worship we must understand why we worship in the first place.

What is the fundamental theology behind the ministry of worship design? What we know and confess most readily, in human form and divine embodiment, is the presence of Jesus Christ, through whom we live. Jesus is *the* pre-eminent theological design, the ultimate union of revelation and medium. Together with God the Creator and the Holy Spirit, Jesus

You don't just throw a bunch of paragraphs together and call it a sermon and you just don't throw a bunch of stuff up on the communion table and say this is going to be meaningful.

— Deb Schmidt
Hutchinson, Kansas

is the theological source for all design and media available for use in worship. The Trinity is the thumb and finger holes of the liturgical palette. It is what worship leaders hold onto as they design worship and worship spaces.

In her brief but sturdy book, *Spaces for Spirit*, Nancy Chinn explores worship through the lens of the visual. With the help of illustrative photographs, she describes the historical role of visual art as a trusted method of conveying religious doctrine. "A visual cue in the cathedral would have either brought up information transmitted orally or prompted a question about its meaning. If you knew the code, you had a shortcut to a complex theological idea."[12] These shortcuts and codes—from literal depiction to abstract representation—are the shared language of biblical word and biblical image.

Chinn then turns to formal elements of design and their role in the praying community. *Color*, she says, is a symbol that locates us in God's time, the mind making quick associations with Pentecost red, say, or Lenten purples. *Transparency* is the design that hints at the presence of something spiritual amidst that which remains concretely visible. Stained glass or sheer fabric, for example are fitting materials for services like baptism and ordination, occasions where the Spirit is overtly summoned. Chinn explores the theological parallels of *light and darkness* (sin and grace), *scale* (how big is God anyway?), and *movement* (analogous to Christian growth). She shows us the nubby *texture* of a diverse community and a global gospel. Of visual *rhythm* and its function in worship, she says that "pattern does for the eye what praying the rosary does for the fingers."[13] (Granted, we may not pray the rosary, but how many of us have traced the panels of cedar behind a preacher's head, or counted organ pipes—hearing little but leaving worship blessed nevertheless?)

Where two or three gather, God is among them. Where God is revealed, creation responds in adoration and earnest praise. The church's worship is the *liturgical palette*. But there is also the *artistic palette*. Here, however inadequately, the formal characteristics of design, the very materials of earth, are taken up and made useful to the purposes of God's self-revelation. Think of Mary and Joseph. The shape of their culture, the color of their skin, the texture of the swaddling clothes, the space where the baby cried—these are the very components of formal artistic design

Sometimes the face of God is revealed in a wagon of canned goods, a tall white candle burning in earnest, or sidewalk chalk on the church's pavement. These are the canons of art and theology. Art as pastoral care acknowledges that frequent carriers of the visual Word are human "dreams, signs, and wonders," imagination and creative hope. If we are to continue moving toward the images of Kingdom life implanted by the gospel in the worshipping com-

Story forward to mix with our stories. It builds community and forms a people as the stories intertwine and as the worship artists invite engagement with the Story across generations.

> *In Lent we had a winding path going up to the front. Along the path we had rocks and potted bare limbs, trees, that sort of lined the path. It was a very simple treatment but as it evolved, the pastor used this winding way telling the children's stories. On Palm Sunday, the entire congregation became the crowd as the children and the parents were making their way down the path with their palm branches . . . It became a theatre in the round in a way that none of us expected when we first designed this.*[21]

. . . the metaphorical

Metaphor is the unlikely pairing of two unrelated things, which we then talk about as though they were continuous and sitting together naturally with relative comfort.

> *We knew for Lent this year we wanted to work with the suggestion of a gradual move to darkness and sort of a movement motif that was circular. We went with a spiral, so we had an Amish craftsman forge an iron black spiral that is about four feet in diameter and that single, black, solitary thing will be hanging from Ash Wednesday on through to Easter Sunday.*[22]

The iron spiral was an image of the circuitous nature of the journey toward repentance. When Easter came, the spiral disappeared, but for the congregation there remained the image of that slow and circular journey. Metaphor, therefore, provides the imagination an image, a place, in which to play with hefty ideas in a realm that is more natural, familiar, or accessible. When the two are again separated, as they need to be, we find the one of primary importance imbued with new meaning for having interacted with the symbolic parallels of another.

. . . the symbolic

Symbols carry deep meaning and point beyond themselves, simplifying the complex. The cross is the pre-eminent symbol of Christian faith, carrying threads of servanthood, discipleship, suffering, and resurrection. We see a chalice and loaf of bread, and the story and the act of communion open before us, full of memory and meaning. We see a basin and towel, and the story and the act of foot washing open before us, full of memory and mean-

. . . to see their visual prayers— shaping the flow of worship and to see other prayers respond to their prayer. It is just this lovely, collaborative movement that happens.

— *Mary Lou Weaver Houser*
Lancaster, Pennsylvania

We declare to you what was from the beginning, what we have heard, what we have seen with our eyes, what we have looked at and touched with our hands concerning the word of life.

— 1 John 1:1-3

ing. Scripture, of course, underlies these large symbols of faith across the church. Rich meanings, also undergirded by Scripture, are often particular to congregational life.

> *We have a tapestry, we call it, that symbolizes our life together, how each of us adds color and texture to the community. [It symbolizes] that it isn't our sameness that holds us together, but Jesus Christ, who is the grid through which we are all woven. We become a body when we allow ourselves to be woven together by the Spirit of Christ. On membership Sunday we have a basket of fabric strips in a variety of colors and textures, so that after each new member gives their testimony, they go to the tapestry and weave in their piece of fabric wherever they want. After that Sunday, we hang it out in the foyer again until the next year.*[23]

. . . the universal[24]

This spectrum of design began with the literal. At the other end of the spectrum lies the universal. Universal design choices are not representational and do no carry specific elements of Story. They are therefore not concerned with "it" as a single, quickly read, identifiable interpretation. Rather, universal design choices address mystery, grapple with the complex, are open to multiple points of entry and interpretation, and invite communal dialogue on the road to transformation.

> *On the wall behind the pulpit, I installed a ten foot banner made of five layers of sheer voile cotton. On each of those layers were head-shaped ovals in the varying colors of humankind . . . In her sermon, the pastor used the analogy of an athletic stadium. Many people told me later that the "eggs" on the banner became the great cloud of witnesses during the sermon that day . . . [a] special eureka moment well earned by the people making the connections between the word and the visual.*[25]

The "cloud of witnesses," that mysterious and wonderful image of the people of God across time and eternity, begins and ends this brief discussion of the spectrum of design. A literal design choice made the cloud visible in empty shoes encircling the worship space. A metaphoric design choice might use a stack of books authored by great theologians and saints through the centuries. A universal design choice accommodated "eggs," incomprehensible as they may have been at the start of the service, to engage imaginations. This allowed interpretations of that "cloud of witnesses" to form as the image fused with the words of the sermon.

Literal, representational, narrative, metaphorical, symbolic, and universal—all are excellent design choices. Each design, with appropriate modes of ritual response, makes way for the Living Word to do what it has always done: to become. Biblical imagery supports ongoing incarnation, for the Word becomes not only flesh but also wisdom, creation, community, and covenant. Our work as worship planners is to hold text and context together, discerning, for this time and this people, that fitting union of revelation and expression, that careful selection of expression that best conveys what God has made known.

liturgical freedom

a new clock

imaginative license

a place of gathering

a wordless sanctuary

a new calendar

a story intricately woven

an engaging mystery

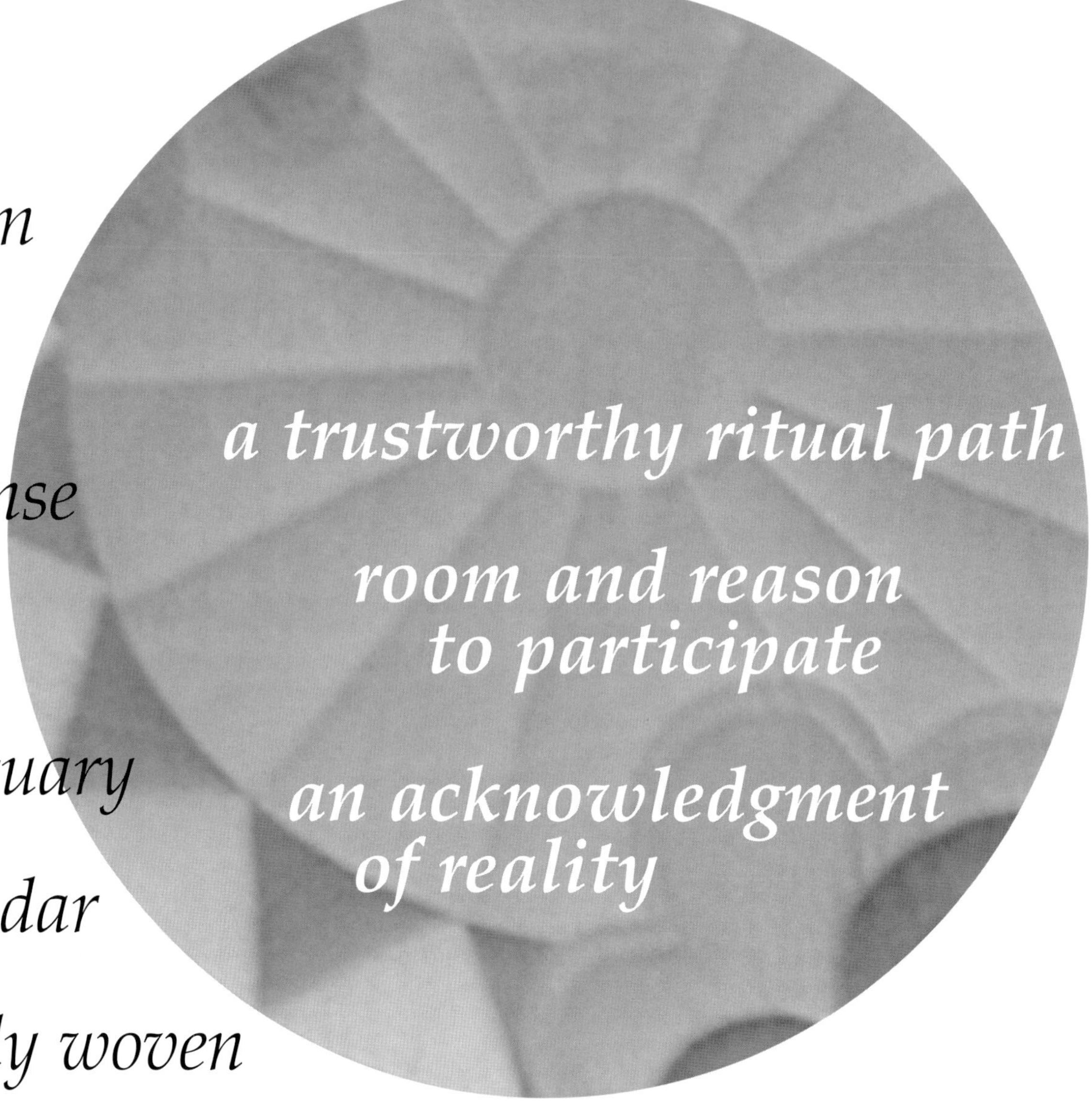

a trustworthy ritual path

room and reason
to participate

an acknowledgment
of reality

and everyday life. These are the corporate signs of distinction; they are who we are becoming and what worship fosters and expects.

The Repetition of Becoming Holy

Inseparable from the habituation of Christian folkways is the feature of repeatability. The regularity of meeting for ritualized patterns of storytelling is our covenantal mandate, given by Jesus: "As often as you meet, do this . . . " (Luke 22:19). If we agree to meet on Sundays we do have repetition. In a secular age of virtual community, high-speed travel, and staggering change, this agreement to meet once a week to do the same thing over and over is a marvel too often overlooked. If we break bread in a biblical pattern, we do have ritual, a "repeated action initiated by Jesus and bearing the promise of his presence."[5]

Honoring Jesus' mandate, coming together repeatedly to retell, remember, and relive the Story, rehearsing in ritual and sacrament that which we will become—these activities form Christian distinctives in the community, fostering a Christian worldview in our historical time and place. Memory binds together those who remember a common story. Symbols in the context of the Story remind us of who we are, where we came from, and how graciously God has dealt with us. Thus, for example, in baptism and communion, water and bread, the mighty correspondence among ritual, symbol, and Scripture comes alive.

Biblical symbols, actively engaged in worship, position themselves ahead of us so that, in time, they become the targets of Christian character. The gospel wants what symbols want—to be spotted and pursued with zeal. Worship sets out the biblical targets and stocks the congregational quiver, making it possible to aim for holiness. Repeated meeting and engagement, as commanded by the Lord in whose name we gather, is critical to the formation of Christian distinctives in the community and to fostering a Christian worldview

It is not unsurprising that early observers of Christianity were not struck by its "religious" (in our privatized sense) qualities—what struck outsiders was the church's "total way of life."

— *Rodney Clapp*
A Peculiar People

A Caveat

Ritual has the power to infuse light into isolation, chaos, and blinding despair. There is, however, a deep-cast shadow. If ritual holds the power to *form*, it also holds the power to *de*form. This danger requires utmost vigilance from those involved in the design and structure of worship. Deformative worship fractures community with hierarchy and exclusion, with gender

How do liturgy and ethics intersect? Put most simply: Christian ethics is a description of the kingdom of God, which is itself seen most clearly in the patterns of activity enfleshed in Jesus Christ. In the patterns of the liturgy we come into contact with those patterns of Christ. Because of this, as we are formed through habitual participation in the liturgy, we grow in our ability to see the world and act in the world as Christians.

— David L. Stubbs
cited in Leanne Van Dyk's
A More Profound Alleluia

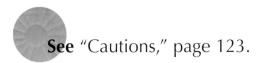

See "Cautions," page 123.

and racial insensitivity. Deformative ritual fossilizes the once-malleable church into a symbol of rigid dogmatism and nostalgia, a place where change is not only unlikely, but unwanted. It is around this concern that suspicion toward repetition—repeated gestures, repetitious liturgy—has its origins. Such wariness, even enmity, may be warranted when proper pastoral care is not taken and worship becomes moralistic, legalistic, ritualistic, or empty.

Worship, for both adults and children, must be free of such "istics." Moral discourse and moral behavior, for example, are definitely worthwhile. But if the children's story prescribes what children are to *do* and neglects calling for imaginative ways to *be* and to *envision* behaviors consistent with Kingdom symbols, we have a *moralistic* sermon. A sermonic form may carry sound moral teaching, but if it robs the community of gracious space for interpretation and appropriation of design, visual or otherwise, it is in danger of moralism. Similarly, an action of worship is *ritualistic* when it bears worthwhile outward features of Christian practice, such as prayer or bread-breaking, but fails to honor the heart of Jesus' teaching or mandate..

Done properly, however, proclamation by design can actually work against some of these pitfalls of deformity. Lighting the Christ candle while confessing disunity in the church, for example, is a powerful ritual that binds diverse viewpoints, creating order through which fair dialogue can flow, transforming the view of individual priorities into the sole vantage point of Jesus, our Lord. Lighting the Christ candle in the midst of great disunity is a rightful profession that Jesus will be the only Lord of our communities. Lighting the Christ Candle, however, in a church that denies its disunity is not only a failure of worship, it is a failure of witness to the watching world.

In its essence, ritual bears the mighty responsibility to foster community, order, and transformation. This trinity is an indispensable gift to the postmodern world in its individualism, moral chaos, and paralyzing fear. When our rituals and symbols are truly and uniquely Christian in their practice—and "istic"-free—we present to the world an environment where God, in Christ, might have God's way in our very sense of belonging, moral expectation, and hope for life-giving change. Attending to both the light and the shadow potential of our sponsorship of formative practices will help our congregations participate in dynamic worship—freely and safely, confidently and unselfconsciously.

True Christian identity, after all, is a corporate identity. The vocation of the body of Christ, reflexed in the folkways of Christ, is likewise corporate. It follows, then, that the formation of identity should occur in the corporate setting of worship. "The pastoral purpose of worship (is) to empower a distinctive people," writes Alan Kreider.[6] Against the individualistic bent of our culture, this corporate nature stands out. Against the shaping symbols and practices of our secular world, the church's story and practices are not only peculiar but, at their most potent, revolutionary. When worship includes distinctive ritual and symbolic acts that nurture a desire to reflect Christian identity in the rest of life, it tends to the work of pastoral care in spiritual formation. It also confronts and counters the ever-present, insistent competing symbols of secular culture.

The Way People Come

The outcomes of the gospel—salvation, reconciliation, justice—lie beyond our ministry, but effective communication of that Story is our task. Proclamation through design is demanding, and requires nothing less than skilled liturgical decision, sustained attention of the assembly, and corporate participation in regular meeting. But alas, how does the church gather? Often, like the disciples of Emmaus, it lacks spiritual vision and is too disheartened to bother looking up.

> *Earlier this week, I was in the sanctuary and did my morning prayers up by the cross. Right there at the window you can hear a lot of road noise, especially at that time of the morning. All of a sudden, I realized it was incredibly quiet and I could hear birds singing. Then, as the traffic returned, I could hear the birds singing—even above the traffic. The birds had been there all along. But, having that moment to become aware, I was then able to stay tuned in. Worship is kind of like that. It helps us . . . tune in and become aware of that which the road noise so often overshadows.*[7]

Road noise is to the deafened spirit what the endless bombardment of secular symbol is to the disheartened church, what Jesus' burial was to the disciples. The gospel isn't getting through. And this is how many people come to (and depart from) worship. To rationalize their discomfort around art in the worship space, leaders will say simply that their church is "visually illiterate." But that is not true. Technology, advertising, and entertainment have left their users trained in visual recognition and symbolic engagement. People with these skills fill our pews and spill from our church doors into the world. Another explanation must be found for the disquietude around liturgical symbolism.

We are not at all visually illiterate. Rather, we are visually overloaded with symbols from our secular culture while being visually deprived of alternative symbols of godly pleasure, peacemaking, and praise. Thus, on a Sunday in January, the church fails to notice that the

In this age of a million choices, we are a remnant, the sometimes faithful, sometimes unfaithful family of a difficult and glorious God, called to seek and proclaim God's presence in a disillusioned world.

—*Barbara Brown Taylor*
The Preaching Life

Humanity is a blinded race and in worship we have a chance to look on the world as it truly is— the beloved and redeemed creation of God the Father, Son, and Holy Spirit.

— *Rodney Clapp*
  A Peculiar People

purple banners of Advent have changed to gold. Though the choir's anthem, "Star of the East," could prompt the celebration of a global gospel, weeks of Christmas carols in the mall have deafened the congregation. Now it doesn't know what to listen for. Blinded, exhausted, and financially depleted by a commercial Christmas, the church fails to attend to the calendar that possesses eternal value. Whose stories are we living, exactly?

Our failure to see Christ in worship, therefore, might be less a fault of the eyes than of the heart—less a failure to see and more a failure to look critically at the secular lie we're being told. Whereas a secular worldview tells us that God is nowhere to be found, a sacramental worldview says that God continues to be revealed, and the designs that declare God's presence are everywhere for the using. Unseen but everywhere visible, this is the God we proclaim. Good worship planning seeks to maintain this double-vision: awareness of the holy, and awareness of the designs that proclaim it best. The design of modern worship said, "close your eyes and pray," or "sit while we preach to you." Postmodern worship says, "Look up and see," and uses a proclamation design that says, "Move about and let's imagine the Story together."

The link between a wholesale acceptance of and participation in the symbols of the dominant culture, and a neglect of biblically-mandated symbols of the church presents a serious pastoral challenge. With the biblical symbols of history rendered powerless in their role as mere decoration—we consistently fail to apprehend the moral and doxological demands they could be making on us. The visual environments of many of our worship spaces are therefore not so much austere as they are silent.

Meanwhile, the church is prompted by advertising (Buy!), reflexed by the news (Fear!), reminded by marketing (Need!), and engaged by entertainment (Relax! Applaud!). It is astonishing how such vast amounts of time and money are offered to the gods of advertising, media, and entertainment while the church remains remarkably indifferent, or even opposed, to that peculiar set of images that stands a chance of forming us into the peculiar folk God intends us to be. For this failure alone, the surrounding culture has reason to rebuke the church. Jesus would not recognize bread that was unfairly distributed or a calendar that failed to center itself in the Story. The church, therefore, is theologically blind, not visually illiterate.

Becoming Through Attentiveness

Perhaps there is something in our culture that inhibits memory or teaches us not to pay attention. Alongside the design of liturgical proclamation there exist many others. Consider the design of the average sit-com, with camera angles changing every three seconds. *Little wonder we can pray for barely this long.* The design of video games allows the consequences of violence to be erased by a reset button. *Little wonder we turn a blind eye to injustice and fail to confess our participation in it.* In the design of consumerism, mere signage makes our mouths water for cheap food with no nutritional value. *Little wonder we crave drive-through sermons, the immediacy of proof-texting, and moralistic preaching. And little wonder that one cube of store-bought bread is enough to satisfy the individualistic faith that feeds on it.* Or consider the design of entertainment, where even news programs titillate with sensational headlines and imagery. *Little wonder our worship spaces are configured like theaters and worship leaders are elevated, amplified, rehearsed, illumined, and even applauded. Little wonder individualized faith feels overwhelmed by images in the news and the demands of consumerism.*

We have evidence in the pew, not only of secular influence but also of religious attention-deficit. This condition is exacerbated when a congregation fails to participate in good worship design, or when worship leaders fail to facilitate such participation. In this time when the church seems increasingly in need of the liturgical arts, an artist's revelry is overshadowed by one sobering pastoral concern: "What if the arts were used only for secular purposes?" The world understands that imagery holds great power in the formation of a people. History reveals many examples of censorship of the arts borne out of fear of the shaping power of the arts. (In the context of the church, we would call this iconophobia. Icon means image, and phobia is whatever spooks us to the point of squeezing our eyes shut.) Yet history also gives many examples of the world using the arts to shape identity. Imagery from some source will form us. The question is, by what images shall we be formed?

> The liturgy provides a guiding horizon that both reframes our questions and guides our thinking in certain directions . . . [It] does provide a normative context in which to do our ethical thinking and acting.
>
> —David L. Stubbs
> cited in Leanne Van Dyk's
> A More Profound Alleluia

Affiliation with Holy People

Perhaps it is time to let secular culture rebuke the church for its censorship of the arts, simply by considering the ways in which believers do *not* fear the arts when they are in secular environments. A person seeking to lose weight joins a dieting program, and begins by telling about her struggles with food, childhood reflexes, and so on. She hears stories of others like

We come together as worshipping communities, not because we are perfect but precisely because we are not. So, week after week, we gather to "draw the holy into life." We expect to hear, to taste, to see, to touch, to remember, and to imagine God in our lives.

— *Janet Walton*
  Postmodern Worship and the Arts

her, finding solidarity in her pursuit to become something other. She now prepares food ritually, under the motivating symbol of renewed health. Likewise, a man joining Alcoholics Anonymous introduces himself at a regular meeting, naming himself and his addiction. Given that the addiction was established through rituals of the substance abuse (taking drinks at certain times and places), the addiction must be ritually destroyed in order that new reflexes might be produced in its place. After five months of sobriety, he receives a key chain, a deeply coded symbol readily recognized by other members of AA.

A community seeking to become Christ-like is similarly covenanted through diverse yet transcendent stories of human experience, confessing the reflexes of early faith and the struggle with those pervasive reflexes called sin and idolatry. The church inscribes itself to a particular set of symbolic folkways, behaving its way toward the Kingdom life symbolized and embodied in Jesus Christ. For this kingdom of peace, baptism reminds us, we must be willing to die, not in combat, but in sacrificial love. We hold regular meetings in the mode of praise and confession, acknowledging who we are in light of who God has revealed Godself to be. God is Holy; we are not. God is community; we are, to varying degrees, fickle and divided. God is covenanted to creation; we are only fitfully faithful. And so it is that, ritually, the church names its addictions and divisions in the presence of a storied community through whom this covenantal God seeks unrelentingly to bind us to God's holy self.

Communion is the one thing the God of Trinity wants to share with us, since we are created in that distinct communitarian image. Communion is who we are becoming. Ongoing communion is the predominant symbol of Scripture. The church simply joins a feast already and forever underway. In our worship, both at the Eucharistic table and beyond, we remember Jesus' communion and we sample heaven's communion. As mission, this same symbol is animated in the church's work of promoting justice and peace. This communion, however, assumes one demanding requirement: participation.

Becoming Through Participation

These windows reveal us as Christians . . . so when new people come—it's weird—but it's a way to tell our story. First, because they are striking and then, because they invite storytelling of who we are and how this came to be. The simplicity of them was a central point and we can't look at them without being reminded. You don't even know what it is that opens you up to worship until you experience it. [8]

You don't even know what it is that opens you up to worship until you experience it. Envision a full worship space. Imagine the spoken, sung, and visual symbols that might evoke the collective memory of God's steadfast love. Now, imagine the people in the act of remembering. Though much might be happening psychologically, little will be visible to the naked eye. If symbol-rich worship is so essential to Christian formation and that formation requires tending, what shall pastors and worship leaders be looking for?

Take that same assembly, however, and imagine it "experiencing" worship, participating in it. Mennonite missionary and avid symphony-goer, Alan Kreider says that, although he is seated and silent until the time of ritual applause, he is every bit engaged in the performance, so much that his body is stiff the following morning. The symphony is Kreider's analogy for participatory worship.[9] Ritual participation, as Kreider describes it, is not necessarily grand pageantry or weekly altar calls, conspicuous gestures, and unison response. Participation in worship simply means folks are awake as opposed to asleep, expectant as opposed to disenchanted, beguiled as opposed to indifferent. The worshipping church is the symphony *and* the audience. In the presence of proclamation, verbal and visual, we can expect to confront God and to be confronted, to bless and to be blessed. This is the effect of good liturgical installation, requiring nothing less than alertness, expectation, and investment. These are the ready qualities of experiential worship and the collective disposition that leaders should be looking for.

Worse than disapproval or disdain, liturgy's greatest challenge is with those who are spiritually snoozing. The irritated ones are, at least, engaged. An anesthetized church, by contrast, has been lulled to sleep by a combination of too many words and not enough participation in worship. In such a space, the church sits on its comfy pew Sunday to Sunday failing to understand why worship is profoundly uninteresting and Monday to Monday wonders what it's all for.

So wake up! Come and see! Come closer still! As you do so, the mighty correspondence between gospel and art can be named again; both crave to be engaged. Scripture wants what art wants: to be seen and handled, to evoke wonder and inspire response. Look hard, wrinkle your nose, handle with eyes and hands. Worship art is installed in liturgy, and by its very name, liturgy requires human handling. We can roam the worship space of First Mennonite all week long. But, says Deb Schmidt, not until we participate in worship will we understand the formative interplay between remembering and rehearsing, the sponsoring of faith. This is the work of pastoral care.

In the liturgy, day to day, and week to week, we "do the world as God means for it to be done." This means that in worship we vigorously enflesh a restored and re-created world—a world returned to its genuine normality through holy abnormality. Worship is not simply world-changing. It is, indeed, world-making.

—*Rodney Clapp*
A Peculiar People

We sometimes speak as if the Bible can be considered the Word of God just because it lies on the page, static and lifeless. If this were the case, we should pass out pieces of paper containing the text for the day, allow for sufficient time for reading, and then dismiss the faithful in silence.

—*Robin R. Meyers*
With Ears to Hear

There is an immensely important sense in which "who we are," waits upon who we say we are. When we perform ourselves, we do not simply express what we already are; we perform our becoming, and become our performing.

—*Joan Carter*
Postmodern Worship and the Arts

The Clumsy Dance Rehearsal of Holiness

Athletic trainers use machines that simulate wind, altitude, and resistance. The body can enter the *simulated* activity in order to be reflexed for the *real* activity. Similarly, aeronautics makes use of cockpit simulators, a convincing environment of weightlessness and projected images that require hypothetical navigation. The machines are not quite a shuttle, but a sampling of the real that expects and fosters the use of well-honed reflexes when it really counts.

The church also has its simulators. The Old Testament calls them festivals and feasts, rituals and offerings. The New Testament baptizes, breaks bread, and washes feet. Anglicans say *liturgy*. Mennonites say *worship*. Corporate worship is "virtual" because, though it samples the Kingdom of God, it is not *quite* the Kingdom of God—not what it will be upon completion. Worship is the gathering of earnest brothers and sisters who, though fallible, remain committed to eating bread and rehearsing what it would be like to live in the sustained harmony of that great Day.

This "not-quite-ness" may be one source of the church's uneasiness around ritual and visual participation. We do come to each symbol as fallible people. We are undeserving as we approach each ritual. Where two or more gather to repeat the Story through word and symbol, there is good reason to fear that God will show up and have God's way with us. This is the effect of imagining the result of "Thy will be done." Pastors see this regularly in the grief and relief that precedes the funeral of people who have lived long and well. They encounter it in the battle of compulsion and resistance that people experience with rituals that require a visible response, such as going forward for anointing with oil.

"But what does it mean exactly?" we ask, fearing we will miss "the point"—as if there could be only one. How will it change me? If corporate ritual behavior arranges exposure with God, and if encounters with God, visual or otherwise, leave whole groups of people inexplicably altered, this anxiety is a good thing. It is indeed a "fearful thing to fall into the hands of the living God" (Hebrews 10:31).

With reverent trembling and good pastoral care, we may be assured that fear and clumsiness are to Christian worship what messiness is to Old Testament ritual. Israel's sin offerings required the splattering blood all over the altar. Offering is a human activity and therefore messy. What visual artists are doing in worship is not so much art-making as it is faith offering. It's a human offering, so it will be messy and clumsy.

Visual art is also incomplete and inadequate, for what design could ever fully proclaim the presence of God? Art is no more God than prayer is a rabbit's foot, yet each symbol-in-motion reminds the assembly, in the best way that the praying artist saw fit, that God is among us. Good pastoral care acknowledges the messiness. It recognizes the anxiety surrounding the offering to be a signal of great reverence, and humbly joins the steps already in motion. In awkward, self-conscious participation we remember "it is exactly because of our clumsiness, our gracelessness, that there is value in seeing the liturgy as dance. It is a rehearsal of the Christian story that takes us through the steps again and again. Doing the steps repeatedly—offering our gifts, passing the peace, and so forth—we learn the dance."[10]

Worship symbols thus share in the very reality they exemplify. Therein lies their value; whether or not they achieve the desired outcome, worship is worth doing. The "make believe" of worship activity is nothing less than the "making belief" of a people. As we learn to be less self-conscious, the symbols of worship become a visible trajectory, pointing to the Kingdom. The rituals of worship become reflex, and the stories of faith, second nature. This is the sum effect of liturgical reminding and imagining, of story and folkway. The Christian perspective and the Christian character that moves us to the fulfillment of the Kingdom are marks of Christian maturity. They require a lifetime of pastoral care. They are distinctives to watch for.

Athletes train. Musicians rehearse. The church worships. These verbs produce behaviors that, in time, are fully embodied by the people who do them regularly. Worship is a collective gathering of Christians-in-training, set within a convincing environment of symbols and words that invites imagination and causes time to stand still so the Spirit might have its way with us. Ritual—patterned public activity—arranges the exposure. Symbols capture our attention. Pastoral care mediates the engagement.

Pastoral Care and the Recognition of Jesus

The cultural problems confronting contemporary pastoral care are myriad. What concerns the liturgical artist are those things that keep the church from recognizing the risen Christ in its midst. The Emmaus story illustrates God's ongoing presence and the transformative effect of imagery in the development of faith. Pastoral worship planning requires this two-fold awareness: awareness of the holy and awareness of design.

For the Emmaus disciples there were, as yet, no Easter hymns, no antiphons declaring

See "Ritual Design" and "Dramatic Symbols," pages 101 and 105.

The visual effect was magnificent, but the real power of the event lay in the movement of people forward with light, itself a symbol of prayer, and that gathering of prayer leading to this symbol of the movement of the Spirit . . . a place was provided, and materials brought to enhance worship were turned loose, and the worshipping Church arrived and the Spirit moved.

— *Frances Ringenberger*
Lombard, Illinois

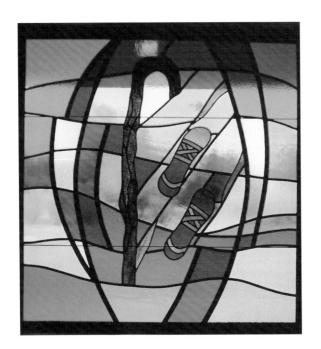

the end of the vigil. The alleluia had been literally buried. The first Easter Sunday was fast losing daylight and with it, purpose and hope. Somewhere along the line the church may have lost heart, lost sight, or lost hope, but the paradigm of the Emmaus story allows us to imagine Christian formation as a round trip from illusion and despair to a glorious return to hope. It invites us to proclaim, again and again, that God is alive and with us. Look closely. Where, exactly, did the journey turn? In the midst of a tangible encounter with Jesus, the Risen Christ.

On similar roads with similar companions, we make our journey as sponsors of faith development. The postmodern church is longing for just such an encounter. Like the disciples in their plea to Jesus, the postmodern church implores, "Stay with us. Let us swallow your bread, finger your wounds, behold your resurrected face." Indeed, there is much, spiritually and culturally, that keeps our eyes from recognizing him. For some, tragedy lies in the not-so-distant past while others make the trek with a chronic sense of fear, doubt, and aimlessness. For most of us, at least once in a while, a sense of restlessness, doubt, or even apathy marks our gait as we wonder whether the Risen Christ still makes appearances.

Together, as coauthors and as just two testimonial voices among many, we say he does.

A Catalogue
of Art Created
for Worship

**Madison
Mennonite Church
Madison, Wisconsin**

Bethel College Mennonite Church
North Newton, Kansas

The Windows of First Mennonite Church Hutchinson, Kansas

The Stuff of Life

"This Do In Remembrance Of Me"

Lenten Journey
Lombard Mennonite Church
Lombard, Illinois

Banners of Shalom Mennonite Church Newton, Kansas

Associated Mennonite
Biblical Seminary
Elkhart, Indiana

Advent
Belmont Mennonite Church
Elkhart, Indiana

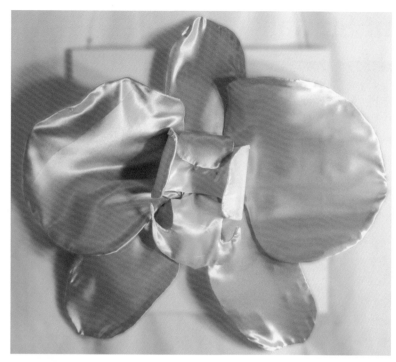

Advent Starfall

Sculpture of LaVerle Schrag

The Arms of God

Lenten Journey
Sunburst

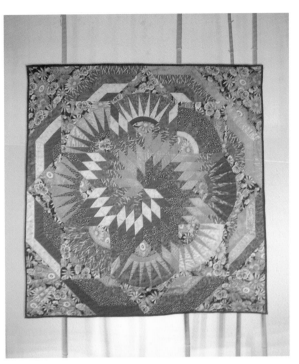

**Lenten Journey
Community Mennonite Church
Lancaster, Pennsylvania**

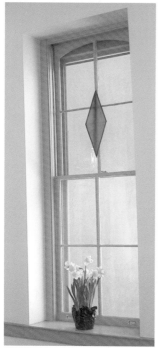

Cut Paper Cross
Hope Mennonite Church
Wichita, Kansas

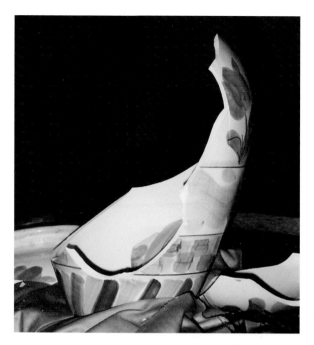

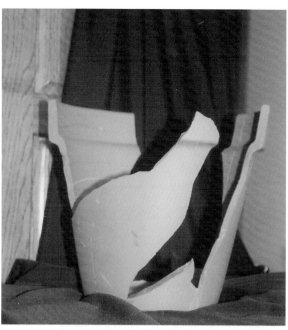

**Broken and Blessed
A Lenten Journey**

The River of God

Flame

Rock

Bread and Cup

"This Do In Remembrance Of Me"

Celebration!

The Studio

In the Liturgical Closet

Every worship closet will have a different look. Time, tradition, the unique life of the congregation it serves, and the repeating cycles of the Christian year will deepen its possibilities, expose its deficits, and invite some rethinking about the objects kept there. Here are some suggestions of things most often needed.

Banner storage	acid-free tubes, in acid-free fabric, PVC pipe, or custom banner rack
Baskets	for special offerings, displays, devotional candles, ritual props
Bible	large altar Bible and podium riser
Candles	in colors of the Christian year, a Christ candle, varying heights and widths. (pillars, tapers, votives, tea lights, devotionals) Butane lighter(s), an ornate snuffer, nylon for buffing, peace candle
Candle holders	floor and tabletop holders for presentation, height, cleanliness and safety.
Catalogues	of available artists and their preferred medium or personal collections of fabric, sculpture, framed art or related objects; fair trade store catalogue, with information about borrowing arrangements with the store
Crosses	varying sizes, textures, media, cultures
Fabric	various colors and textures, solids and patterns, ethnic designs, quilts; storage for large—folded on shelves or rolled on doweling; storage for small—folded in dresser drawers or multiple pant hangers; storage for silk—in zippered storage bags

Florals	flowers and plants
Lanterns	oil, wick, funnel
Naturals	objects such as rocks, twigs, branches, wheat
Paraments/ vestments	for vesting furniture, walls, worship leaders
Pillars	floor pillars of varying heights, draped with fabric or left as natural wood
Pottery	chalice and plate set, basin, pitcher, bowls, platters, candleholders
Risers	tabletop risers of varying heights, draped with fabric or left as natural wood
Ritual supplies	oil for anointing, ashes for imposition, sand for devotional candles
Sandbox	made of Plexiglas, on castors; for devotional candles, children's worship
Sculpture	classical, contemporary; may include a catalogue of sculpture found in congregational homes
Stands	tabletop stands or easels for plaques, icons, pictures, framed art, books

The common elements of earth, air, fire and water, and the fruits of the earth and human work—oil, wheat become bread, and grapes become wine, ordered sound and visual form—all are symbolic and communicative power when used in Christian worship.

—*Don E. Saliers*
  Arts, Theology, and the Church

Hardware and Maintenance

Candle care	wax trimming container, discard box for used matches, knife, piece of nylon fabric for buffing
Camera	to catalogue installed art and available materials
Fabric care	hamper, iron, ironing board, spray bottle, spray starch, lint roller, fusible web for quick repairs and hems
Installation kit	pins, stapler, glue gun, measuring tape, hammer, tacks, eye hooks, level, butane lighter and matches, dowel rods, fishing line, awl,

screwdrivers, utility knife, self-sticking Velcro, double-sided tape, packing tape, various lengths of cable ties, side cutters, wire, small freezer bags of fine sand for elevation or softening corners, wagon or cart for transport

Surface care   wood polish, glass cleaner, soft cloth

 # Scale and Placement

A long walk   As you build your worship closet, a periodic walk around the worship space is helpful to make sure objects used in your worship space are big enough that the important details can be seen from all around the room—from the back seats, the far sides of the sanctuary, from the balcony. Things that read very well in the average living room can be lost in the worship space.

Time to sit   Before leaving the space, sit in different locations across the sanctuary to see things as worshippers will see them on Sunday morning.

The Liturgical Year

With Christ's life and ministry at its heart, the liturgical year helps us retell, remember, and relive the stories that form us as a people of the Word, pulling the Story forward and letting it mix with our story. Stories intertwined, we live out of a sense of time and season that marks our faith.

The season of Advent

The liturgical year begins with Advent, a season that extends across the four Sundays prior to Christmas. It is a season of preparation and anticipation, looking for *Christ, the longed for Messiah* (Luke 4:78-79), both as Incarnation and as Risen Christ coming again. Some of the most evocative texts of our Story are at the heart of Advent—texts that reveal God at work, and texts of preparation, recognition, and receiving—making it a season for seeing, hearing, touching, and imagining. The season is marked by the lighting of Advent candles each week in anticipation.

The season of Christmas

A celebration and praise of *Christ, the Word made flesh and dwelling among us* (John 1:14), Christmas is a season that lasts 12 days.

The season of Epiphany

The word *epiphany* means manifestation, and in the liturgical calendar it focuses on *Christ, the Light of the world* (John 8:12)—including among Gentiles, as symbolized by the magi. Beginning as a celebration on January 6th and ending with the beginning of Lent, it is a season of service and response. The day is symbolized by light. The season highlights witness.

The season of Lent

Lent is the second season of preparation and is characterized by penitence and prayer, reflection and renewal, identifying with *Christ, who walked among us* (John 3:16-17). Reading, study, prayer, meditation, and examen (self-inventory) are the spiritual practices highlighted during Lent, a rich time for formation in community and discipleship. During Lent, services often end with prayer for the people instead of with a blessing. "Alleluias" are absent from worship—suspended until the joyful time following Easter.

Holy Week

This special week moves from the triumphant entry of Palm Sunday, toward the cross with *Christ, the Suffering Servant, the Lamb of God* (Isaiah 50:4-9a, John 1:29). The institution of the Lord's Supper and Christ's New Commandment (John 13:34-35) are observed on Maundy Thursday, often with a meal, communion, and/or foot washing. The passion and suffering of Christ on the cross are shared on Good Friday with a solemn reading of John 18:1—19:42. In some traditions, the worship space is stripped and emptied, and no other services are held until Easter. Other traditions observe Holy Saturday, a day of lost hope, silence, and emptiness marking Christ's time in the tomb.

The season of Easter

The high point of the liturgical year is the proclamation of *Christ, our Resurrected Lord* (John 20:19) on Easter Day. The season of Easter continues for 50 more days and highlights the renewed promise revealed in Christ's post-resurrection appearances. "Alleluias" burst back into our worship and starkness is replaced with color and joyful expressions in art and music. The paschal mystery of Christ's death and resurrection are joined with Christ's ascension and the coming of the promised Spirit to God's people.

The season of Pentecost

The season of Pentecost is the longest of the liturgical year. A season of service and response, it begins on Pentecost Sunday, celebrating the coming of the promised Spirit of Truth (John 15:26-27). The first Sunday after Pentecost, Trinity Sunday, celebrates the full revelation of the God we praise, the Christ we follow, and the Spirit indwelling. In the long season of Pentecost we look to *Christ, the Pioneer and Perfecter of our faith* (Hebrews 12:2), our guide for ministry and model in life. The season of Pentecost ends on Christ the King Sunday, the Sunday just prior to Advent. Here, we look back across the year to see the whole Story we have experienced together in our own story, acknowledging Christ to be King of Kings and Lord of Lords.

The Colors
of the Liturgical Year

The seasons of the Christian year are marked by the use of colors. Over time, the colors come to be understood and treasured in the life of the assembly, connecting us to sisters and brothers in the broader church who also observe this tradition. Using the traditional colors can be freeing, setting some parameters at the start of worship planning. As we build a worship closet of fabrics that can be used again and again, we are free from the temptation to decorate the worship space with trendy color schemes or favorite combinations.

While the white and gold of celebration and the red of Pentecost have a more limited range, the colors of the other seasons lend themselves to greater range of interpretation. The green of Ordinary Time, for example, doesn't always have to be bright and clear. Other greens, from sage to forest, can enliven the long, changing season of Ordinary Time. Blues and purples should always be strong, but a midnight blue might be used instead of a brighter blue; and purples range from those with more red to those with a decidedly bluish hue. A rule of thumb is that colors should be true to the spirit of the seasons they represent. Darker, more somber colors work well in seasons of preparation; pure, bright, rich colors are appropriate for seasons of celebration; and the many shades and hues of green that are the colors of growth and hope in the seasons of response.

Blue: The color of Advent has traditionally been purple, but blue is often used for this first season of the Christian year. Using blue helps to differentiate Advent from Lent and invites a sense of mystery, wonder, and anticipation as we await the coming of Christ. Advent candles, one lit each Sunday of the season, should also be blue or purple. (Where purple candles are used, a rose candle is traditionally lit on the third Sunday of Advent. This Sunday is known as Gaudete Sunday because the word *rejoice* [*gaudete* in Latin] in the readings for that Sunday.)

I didn't grow up with liturgical colors or even a church year, for that matter. I'm finding it really intriguing and a great spark of creativity to have the constraints of the liturgical year and the colors.

—*Esther Kreider Eash*
Wichita, Kansas

White/Gold: These are the colors for times of celebration. Some congregations use only white at such times, but might add gold at Easter. Other congregations use both gold and white as their celebration colors.

- **Christmas Season:** Since everything around us screams red and green, the temptation will be strong to use these colors in worship. Try to keep white (and possibly gold) prominent. When Advent candles have been used, a large white candle, representing Christ's presence, should be added on Christmas. This candle will be lit throughout much of the coming Christian year.
- **Easter Season:** For this most important season of celebration be lavish with your use of white and gold. Rich color, provided by real flowers, adds to the sense of joy and celebration.
- **Epiphany, Baptism of the Lord, Transfiguration, Trinity, and Christ the King** are single days of celebration in the life of Jesus. Since they are single Sundays, it is tempting not to mark them by changing the color to white. It's worth the time, though, because these days are the Christ-focused brackets to the seasons of response or, at Epiphany, celebrate Christ as the light of the world.

Purple, the color of Lent, serves as a foundation for symbols of barrenness and brokenness. The worship space may be stripped of all other color and signs of life. Plants and flowers are not used during the season. Purple is the traditional color for Lent, but in some faith traditions the use of natural fabrics of brown, beige, or gray are used instead. Congregations that use purple at Advent should take care to use different hues at Lent.

Green, the color of life and growth, is used for both seasons of Ordinary Time, "the time of the church" that occurs between the other seasons. The second season of Ordinary Time, the season of Pentecost, is long, from late spring to late fall. Greens chosen for this lengthy season can shift as the seasons of the natural world changes hues.

Red, the color of fire, symbolizes the Holy Spirit. The red should be vibrant and pure. Often, candles in abundance are part of the visual focus on Pentecost.

Scarlet is for the first days of Holy Week, beginning on Palm/Passion Sunday and continuing through Maundy Thursday. The color is deep and rich, and meant to remind us of the depth of Christ's suffering.

Liturgical Color Wheel

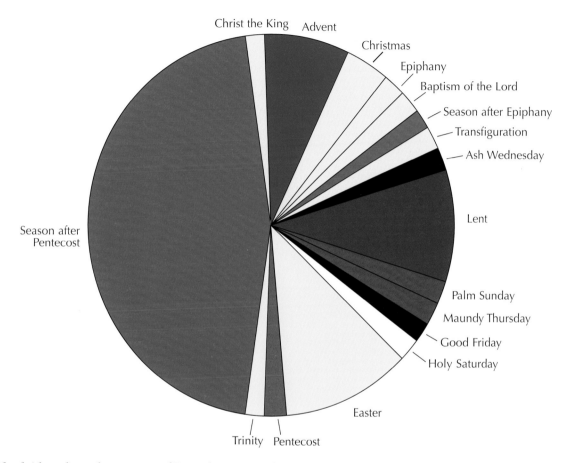

Black * brackets the season of Lent, being used on Ash Wednesday and Good Friday. It speaks of mortality and mourning. Ashes, created from the palm fronds of the previous Palm/Passion Sunday, are the predominant symbol of Ash Wednesday and are placed on the forehead or hand in the shape of the cross as a reminder that we are dust and to dust we will return. The cross itself is the predominant symbol on Good Friday as we remember and enter into Christ's death. Few congregations hold Holy Saturday services, but this is the one day of the Christian year when no color or image should predominate. Holy Saturday is a day of emptiness, sorrow, and longing.

---

*See note 14 of Chapter 3, page 133.

A Spectrum of Design:

That which words present to us through hearing, art silently reveals to us in image.

—*St. Basil the Great*

As metaphor, art in the place of worship, at the service of the community, can be used to evoke, to help the soul dance between mood and idea, between experience and prayerful reflection on that experience.

—*Nancy Chinn*
   Spaces for Spirit

	Literal	Representational	Narrative
Description	A=A • obvious meaning • one-to-one correspondence • common sense • limited interpretation • informational • concrete	A=A1 • stylized or iconic presentation of idea • sign stands for original • mirror of idea in action • translation of idea into different medium	A › B › C › D • progressive development of action • plot
How the concept is presented	Matter of fact • unadorned • straightforward • uncomplicated • explains how things are, • tells it like it is	Illustration of idea • demonstration of concept	Story • unfolds • develops • becomes more complex
What the congregation does	Receives what is given • hears what is said • sees what is presented • accepts what is given • gains information	Sees connection between idea and new medium • enacts the translation	Follows the action • feels the story's tensions and resolutions • senses the story's significance
What the presentation yields	Expanded information • foundational faith vocabulary • basic concepts	Capacity to put a basic idea into action • to translate one experience into another	Common story • shared faith • identity • character formation • worldview (though often unconscious)
What the congregation experiences	Shared knowledge • shared meaning • explanations of essential matters of faith	Participation in idea through imitation • creation of inner desire and intention • sympathy • empathy	Entry into the story • suspension of disbelief • new possibilities for personal stories • redefined ending

Visual Proclamation in the Worshipping Assembly

Metaphoric	Symbolic	Universal	
A is like B • concept set in a relationship with image, object, or experience • insight arises from comparison	**A=B+C+D+E+F** • condensed clusters of meaning • objects, themes, actions take on multivalent meanings • often multisensory	**An=BxCxDxExF** • experience of wholeness • transcendence • sense of expansion, union with all of life • felt experience of grace, love, shalom, etc.	**Description**
As a relationship • parable • analogy • poem	**Complexes of meaning** • signified by codes (i.e., significant words, images, objects, gestures, actions) • opened through the senses	**Interaction of scripture, foundational beliefs, expressive arts (particularly music), and ritual action**	**How the concept is presented**
Observes relationship • considers • analyzes • reconsiders shared characteristics • discerns relevance	**Participates in the symbol** • enters the condensed meanings • gains access to the variety of possible meanings • symbols • interprets collective meaning	**Experiences disclosure of the triune God** • epiphany • revelation	**What the congregation does**
Aha!" • surprise • insight • new way of understanding	**Participation in the multiple dimensions of faith** • active engagement • ignited imaginations • collective and personal meaning	**Transcendent meaning** • integration of thought, feeling, and action • unity • shared community	**What the presentation yields**
New perspective or possibilities • expanded sense of God, self, or world	**Self transcendence** • access to reality (God) beyond the obvious, sensible level of experience	**Congregational and/or personal transformation** • *kairos* • depth of meaning • glimpses of fulfillment (e.g., fulfilled reign of God, unity in the Spirit, unending heavenly worship)	**What the congregation experiences**

A symbol can never be fully defined; its deepest meanings are discovered by maker, by viewer and in context.

—*Nancy Chinn*
Spaces for Spirit

There is a sense that the visual helps us to see anew or see things that we haven't seen before or understand things in a new way that we haven't understood before.

—*Pauline Steinmann*
Saskatoon, Saskatchewan

Setting up a Visual Arts Ministry

Getting Started

Gather with those in your congregation who have a vision for developing visual art in worship. Share your dreams and ideas about how and where your ministry will fit most comfortably and effectively into worship planning in your congregation. A visual arts ministry may take many forms, but the more fully integrated it is with worship planning, the better. Looking toward this goal, consider the following questions:

- How is worship planning done in your congregation? Does it rest primarily with the person preaching? With a standing worship committee? Seasonal planning groups? Are segments of worship spread across several groups?
- Will visual arts ministry be an independent group? A subcommittee under worship committee? Fully integrated into worship committee?
- Is there already a worship budget? How is it utilized? Who has access to those funds?
- Would a visual arts ministry be a structural change, an expansion, or an adaptation within the existing structure? How are structural changes accomplished in your congregation?
- Will your visual arts ministry have responsibility in the congregation beyond worship services, such as other visual installations in the building?
- Who might also share your dream? Invite them to join you.
- Determine a good "first" project. Advent or Lent make good places to start. Denominational materials can help prime the pump as you consider designing visuals appropriate for the season, for your congregation, in your space.

Some Keys to Success

- Start slowly. Give yourselves time to learn.
- Involve members of the congregation.
- Always plan visuals specifically for your space and your congregation. If you borrow visual art ideas, make sure they fit your context.
- Collaborate, collaborate, collaborate! Build community through and with your art.
- Don't hesitate to seek additional expertise or help when you need it.
- Pay attention to the responses to your work. Listen for stories. Invite feedback.
- Evaluate your work as it has unfolded in the context of worship.
- Understand the art as integral to worship, not apart from it.
- Understand your work as ministry—within the group and within the congregation.

It all needs to be about bringing us into God's presence and helping us be aware of God.

—*LaVerle Schrag*
Hutchinson, Kansas

Building Your Ministry

- **Document your work.** Keep notes of ideas, techniques, supplies and suppliers, measurements and structural considerations, costs, etc. Take pictures of worship centers and installations, including changes that are made to the visuals during a season or a series.
- **Look beyond the high seasons.** Make sure you consider visual art that can play an important role for Ordinary Time or during a special sermon series.
- **Define your ministry.** Set goals. Dream dreams. Establish parameters. Develop guidelines. Map relationships within your congregation's structure. Open lines of communication.
- **Secure funding.** Art does cost, whether in actual cash or in materials. You may begin with the enthusiasm and donated materials of those doing the art. As your ministry becomes more integral to your worship, identify sources of funding that will allow the visual arts to continue and to grow. Possibilities include:
  - › individual members underwriting a season or a series
  - › a line in the church budget for at least part of the costs
  - › activities that will raise funds while also raising the congregation's awareness of visual art, even as the events build community and enhance outreach opportunities.

Art allows us to participate in the mystery. It reveals at the same time that it hides. As it unfolds, the mystery deepens.

—*Karen Stone*
Image and Spirit

- **Communicate/educate regularly** through the congregation's newsletter, website, and educational activities:

With children:
  › Help them recognize the colors of the Christian year and the symbols of the Christian faith so they can enter more deeply into worship.
  › Sponsor a children's fair of art created around a particular topic, such as part of a curriculum segment or mission project. Display their art and help the artists price and sell their work for a related cause.
  › Hold a summer art week. Ask artists from your congregation or community to teach. Ask students to plan and create art for an upcoming worship series. Celebrate their contribution to the congregation's worship life when the art is installed.

With adults and youth:
  › Plan a Sunday school or mid-week session at the start of a major liturgical season, introducing them to its art.
  › Consider a longer Sunday school series or mid-week series on faith and art in the past and present.
  › Create a periodic or permanent gallery where members can share their art with one another and encourage the exploration and creation of art.
  › Invite artists from across the broader church to share their art and faith.

Planning Pearls

Some suggestions for text, context, and pastoral care

The Text

- Read, read carefully, and read again—not just the specific verses but those before and after the text to take in the whole story.
- Read from several translations.
- Read it aloud.
- Read it, not just today, but over time. Start early.
- Ask questions:
  › What kind of literature is it—poetry, story, parable, letter?
  › Does the passage use metaphor or symbolism? How?
  › What words or strong verbs pop off the page?
  › What colors or shapes or images come to mind?
  › How might these things be important to your planning?
- Study tools, such as Bible dictionaries, atlases, and handbooks can help with customs, objects, and symbols.
  › Contour the passage:
    Instead of a paragraph or column . . . break the passage apart and rearrange it according to common words and forms. In the end it will look like a poem, with regular indents and groupings. Contouring helps us see how the writer shaped the text in the first place; it also helps us study the overall shape in small segments revealing important connections we might otherwise have missed.
    —Lois Siemens, Kerrobert, Saskatchewan

If the preaching they hear is effective, it will not hand them sacks of wisdom and advice to take home and consume during the week, but invite them into the field to harvest those fruits for themselves, until they become preachers in their own right. Preaching is not something an ordained minister does for fifteen minutes on Sundays, but what the whole congregation does all week long; it is a way of approaching the world, and of gleaning God's presence there.

—Barbara Brown Taylor
The Preaching Life

In the liturgy, in our worship, we are not simply presented with information, much less simply being entertained; rather, we are being made into Christians— our actions and lives are being linked to the life of the world, our hearts to the heart of God, our minds to the Truth.

— *David L. Stubbs*
  A More Profound Alleluia

The narratives of Scripture were not meant to describe our world . . . but to change the world including the one in which we now live.

— *Stanley Hauerwas*
  cited in A More Profound Alleluia

The Context

Remember that you are pulling the biblical Story forward to mix with the story of your particular congregation in a particular place.

- With what significant events or issues is the congregation dealing?
- How does the worship space invite, impair, or influence design choice?
- What about the physical characteristics of the region?
- What are long-held traditions and important symbols in the congregation? For example, are there visual elements that should reappear at Advent or Lent?

Making the Pastoral Connection

Worship planned pastorally is mindful of these questions:

- **Habituation:** What is it about our culture that has trained us to miss glimpses of the Risen Jesus?
- **Rehabituation:** What features of worship might tutor the church in keener observation, awareness and attention?
- **Maturation:** What role does vision have to play in the formation of morality? How is the moral imagination fostered in worship?
- **Transformation:** What is it about our selection of ritual and symbol that transforms both our corporate self-understanding and our worldview?
- **Vocation:** What vantage point shall we adopt in our pursuit of social justice and peace? Do we stand at the centers of power or on the margins?
- **Distinction:** What perspectives are uniquely Christian and distinct to our denomination?

Ritual Design—
Symbols in Motion

Christian Rituals Are . . .

. . . baptism. Like no other ritual, baptism signifies community, order, and transformation. It is so powerful in its effect that it can only be understood through the metaphors of death and rebirth. The self dies in Christ and is reborn as a member of Christ's body, signifying a transformation so profound that it will—or ought to—draw to itself the persecution of the world.

. . . communion. Ritual requires people to show up. When people show up for food rituals (hunting, gardening, preserving) everyone has enough and few eat too much. Communion is a ritual requiring people to show up for nourishment, a table of beggars telling other beggars where the bread is to be found. It is a politically subversive act that announces, through worship, that we have reconciled to the point of eating together despite our differences, pursuing justice to the point of extending all tables in the name of Christ.

. . . prayer. Artists talk about the malleable state of clay as "open time," the time available for shaping material according to the artist's design. Prayer is a ritual of open time where our will is softened in worship, subject to a shaping community that seeks to conform itself to the will of God. The result of prayer is the keen awareness of God's sovereignty.

. . . singing. Music is the ritual of choice for Mennonites because it fits so well their theology of shared vocation. Compatibility between the design and the theology is seen in the unification of voices—harmony in diversity—and embodied Scripture. Music becomes a song that precedes us in the ministry of reconciliation.

... *silence.* People experience periods when prayer, even corporate prayer, is impossible. Not everyone can sight-read the tenor line. Not always can everyone come to the table. Silence is that one ritual, meeting all criteria of liturgy, in which everyone can participate. If spoken worship creates the imaginary hedges of a labyrinth, silence is the spacious path we travel to meet God at the center.

... *proclamation.* Clues that we are in a ritual space are sometimes indicated by the symbols or objects we use in their performance—a table for communion, a pitcher and basin for baptism, rings for a wedding, or a casket for grieving. The pulpit is the furnishing of a tradition whose preferred ritual is proclamation of the Word. Proclamation by design calls people in such a tradition also to make use of the piano, the communion table, a dance, or a flame of red that declares that the Spirit is among us.

Christian Ritual Is . . .

... *magical but not magic.* Ritual does something. It changes people, perceptions, identities, definitions. It is a time set apart for contemplation and reordering. It is communal, and essential for sustainable growth in community. It evokes the powers of a sovereign God and encounters with God leave people changed. Though "magical" in the sense that participants leave altered, the change is carefully initiated and tended by the powers of God and God's community. "Somehow" is a common preface to a story that recounts a ritual encounter with God. Listen for it.

... *efficacious but not mechanized.* Cultural organizations know the effect of symbol and symbols-in-motion and boldly employ rituals to meet the purposes of their agenda. This should never be the church's practice. The church should never "employ" ritual, disguise it as worship, and exploit it even for the desired outcomes of making a people more hospitable, more just, more socially conscious, more missional. This is an abuse of liturgy and a manipulation of its people. Ritual's only purpose is to glorify God. It is at God's initiative alone that the social, political, and moral imprints of these acts of worship are brought to bear.

... *scary but unavoidable.* Ritual requires vulnerability, even leading to a sort of "ritual anxiety." Yet it is through ritual that human beings express the feelings and beliefs for which

[The worshippers] need enough information to participate. If the ritual is short, I keep the instructions short. If the ritual happens to be more complicated, I give instruction in stages.

— *Lois Seimens*
Kerrobert, Saskatchewan

words are wholly inadequate. What matters is that the rituals we perform evoke the power of God and the participation of Christ in this ongoing work of practicing holiness. Ritual is a method of change, but it is God's method, not ours.

Thresholds and Crossroads of Ritual

Separation. If ritual marks a type of gateway, then walking through it is a method of indicating and affecting the transition from a former way to a new way. It's alright to walk through, leaving the old way behind. We walk together.

Incorporation. If ritual is a type of threshold, then what greets the ritual participants is a new way of being and belonging on the other side. It's okay to pass over; there is a community waiting on the other side, ready to welcome us in!

Times in between. If ritual is a safe and hospitable spot to dwell between identities, between decisions, between communities, between names, then it's okay to sit a while. A bridge spans a valley with a sheltered bench at its middle. Ritual is a passage, a shelter, a resting place. The clocks tick differently here, and others are waiting too.

Commemoration. If ritual is a crossroad, certain markers will be left along the way. Marks are left in tears, laughter, testimony, vows, gestures, words, silence, symbols, decision, understanding, reconciliation, healing, community, and ultimately, liberation. It's fine to stand at the intersection for a while. The rest of us are there to watch for traffic.

Ritual Symbols as Pastoral Care

Reconciliation. A congregation divided in controversy finds itself unable to move beyond the description of "the issue." In time, it seems the terminology is more divisive than the issue itself. Ritual offers a moment that is light on words and set apart from the din of discussion. At the annual Agape Love Feast people kneel before a partner at a basin of water. Though the issues remain, the people glimpse a hope that leads to reconciliation in the months to come. (Zion Mennonite Church, Swift Current, Saskatchewan)

Healing. Red helium balloons during children's time help to recount the story of Paul and Silas, illustrating the liberating love of God. One balloon is released while the rest remain attached to the pulpit for visual effect. During congregational sharing, a man describes progress in the treatment of his wife's cancer. Through tears, he struggles to tear the ribbon holding down a balloon. Through tears, the congregation watches. Someone produces a scissors and sharing time continues until the entire ceiling is speckled with red balloons. (Belmont Mennonite Church, Elkhart, Indiana)

Mission. A growing congregation discerns the need to build. Location is an issue, given the church's strong neighborhood presence. Prayer becomes the ritual counterpart to blueprint consultation. The congregation sells its building and purchases land across a parking lot next to the old building. A sycamore stands on the building site. Cutting it down is the reverent ritual of creating wood for the new pulpit, communion table, and paneling in the pastor's office. Before the carpet is laid, families scrawl Scripture texts on concrete, drywall, and studs. (Once you know the story it is impossible to sit in that space and not feel surrounded by blessing.) On Dedication Sunday, a procession begins at the former church. Twelve deacons carry twelve stones, congregants carry hymnals, and children carry toys from the nursery. It is a building made for ritual, a building ritually made. (Belmont Mennonite Church, Elkhart Indiana)

Dramatic Symbols

In the lap of proclamation

The church's symbolic posture for prayer: eyes closed in attention, hands folded to ensure inactivity, head bowed in reverence. The church's emblematic posture for singing: on its feet for good breath support, pairs of people united by the book between them, symbolizing their common theology of praise and witness. But what is the posture for Scripture reading? Given our symbol-laden Scriptures, what room do our worship designs leave for congregational participation? Responsiveness, after all, is the desire of all liturgy.

Early Scripture reading was story-telling. Jewish temple-goers knew their responsive role to be highly participatory as they retold their story and were formed by the story's symbols. But over the centuries, as the gospel "went global," the very nature of proclamation shifted from storytelling to argument. Whereas storied symbols produced engagement, the intended response of argument is agreement. And so, despite myriad liturgical choices, the sermon, delivered in its preferred medium of voice to a passive audience, has superseded all others in the modern protestant tradition.

In a Postmodern world there must, once again, be room for other equally important forms of proclamation, particularly the visible, participatory, and theatric forms. Relying heavily on prominent scriptural symbols, dramatic proclamation sets ancient symbols in motion, which by design, evokes imagination and requires interpretation. Drama places the church in the lap of Scripture, a child of two thousand years of selecting stories from the same 66-volume set. This is the narrative we have chosen to shape us, and we are most susceptible to its corporate shaping power when we worship together. As children of God, we are eager to hear God's voice—participants in the stories that shape our belief.

If we wish to experience life as God intends it to be, we need to see the world as young children do, with imagination and love, seeing and experiencing reality on many levels all at once and never being lulled into believing that what we can name and measure is all there is.

—*Pam Driedger*
Altona, Manitoba

From the start, our worship, fellowship, and mission have held visual symbol as an integral part of who we are, how we connect with God, each other, and all of creation, and what we offer to the community.

—*Randall Spaulding*
Sarasota, Florida

The Cast Shadow of Drama in Worship

As we borrow from terms of the theatre—audience, theatrics, performance—a word of caution is in order. As apt as theatre is as a metaphor for the reenactment of ancient scripts, we must test it for its appropriateness in Christian worship. Though the platform in the worship space is elevated, it is not a stage in the theatrical sense. Though a group has gathered, it is a congregation, which should never to be seen or treated as an audience. If an audience is to be named, may it be God and God alone. The worship leader functions as a pastor or priest, not a master of ceremonies. Though we may appreciate the presentation, the fitting response is vertical, not horizontal.

To illustrate: A Nigerian women's choir smiled graciously through the applause of their first number. "If the performance leads you to praise, then may God be praised," they explained. "We would be glad, instead of applause, for you to lift your hands to the Lord." After the second song and every one thereafter, this gathering of conservative Mennonites raised their hands. The silence was deafening.

Examples of Dramatized Scripture and Pastoral Care

Symbols that challenge. A group of children, close enough to the storyteller to feel a part of the Scripture, see Jesus portrayed by a known outcast in the congregation. Maybe, just maybe, their perceptions of authority will shift to the inclusion of the "least of these."

Symbols that call. A man, struggling with vocation, hears the call of God. In the first person, God speaks from Scripture in a woman's voice amplified in the balcony. Reminded of the prayerful wisdom of his grandmother, his course becomes apparent.

Symbols that summon. A person of an ethnic minority with a heavy accent plays the part of Ruth, and for the first time a congregation understands the cost of saying, "Your people will be my people." Within two years they renovate the community room, opening it to the neighborhood under the name "Naomi's Place."

Symbols that inspire. Bored with prayer for more than ten years, a woman in her thirties closes the living room curtains and dances with God. She had seen a spontaneous dance offered as a prayer of response to the weekly congregational sharing.

Symbols that unify. On Palm Sunday, pairs of deacons—one with a bowl, the other with a fir branch—splatter the congregation with drops of water while they sing "Wade in the Water." Some have to wipe their glasses, people laugh. The page in their songbook is forever wrinkled and nobody cares.

Symbols that attend. So thoroughly prepared is the person portraying the psalmist that he is free to respond to the emotional outpouring of the congregation. Unplanned, he proceeds down the aisle in character with pastoral tenderness, making compassionate contact with the people and never once losing his place in the text.

Dramatic Designs

Characterization: climbing inside Scripture

We call it the Living Word but the characters are not alive. Imagine them, Old and New Testament characters, as empty costumes. We climb inside and re-animate them, let Jesus touch and heal them, forgive and feed them. The theatrical name for this design is characterization, getting into the skin, the mind, the motivation of a character. The theological design is one with vast potential for moral formation as we take on the virtues of biblical characters and their redemptive encounter with God in Christ, the Living Word.

Memorization: Scripture climbing inside us

A woman wades barefoot into a stream of blue cloth, a bucket on her hip. She flicks a bug from a garment, laughing at John's diet. Bent from the hips, she recounts John's ministry, plunging towels as he did people. By the time she's done flapping water from a light tunic, God's voice has descended in a visible blessing. She wrings it out and smells it with delight: "God's beloved," she says, "well pleased." The dramatist has fully memorized the text; it lives in her. Formal drama production requires memorization. So did ancient temple practice. Should it be required still? In theological terms, seeing God in a garden, hearing the Spirit in the laundry room, feeling Jesus in the touch of a friend reflects a sacramental worldview. Imagine how different a day would be if Scripture lived inside what we saw.

Art has the possibility of opening to us, in visible form, mystery. The first way to unlock the mystery, and unlock is not the word either, is by looking and looking and looking—and by entering into that mystery with our own creative response and being grasped by it.

—*Karen Stone*
Image and Spirit

We widen the embrace of those whom we include in our worship when we include the arts.

— Elsie Rempel
Winnipeg, Manitoba

Animation: Scripture with a life of its own

You pull up beside a throbbing car. Contained by windows, the sole occupant throws out his chin, sings along, and sways to the beat, shaking the car's side panels. He's indifferent to the display. He knows the words. Coming to worship with memorized Scripture is like tuning into a favorite radio station. When we know the words we will not be preached at, but will proclaim along! We will also have the bodily freedom to respond—to dance our way to communion, to sway to the sounds of Exodus, to lift holy hands in the presence of God's declared beauty.

Systematization: following a Scripture calendar

Providing a rich, varied, and sustaining biblical diet for a congregation is an important responsibility of pastors and worship leaders. The Revised Common Lectionary, though not the only Scripture calendar, is one way of structuring this exposure. An ordered system of selected Bible readings, the lectionary provides four texts for every Sunday over a three-year period. The four readings are drawn respectively from the Old Testament and Psalms, the Epistles (including Revelation), and the Gospels. A balanced scriptural diet ensures a unified witness to the whole story of salvation, announced and initiated in the Old Testament, fulfilled and proclaimed in the New.

Safety: A Primer

Allergies. Be attentive to fragrances in candles and fresh bouquets.

Breakables. Package them in storage containers, handle with care, report damage, dispose of glass and broken pottery with care.

Climbing. Secure all climbing apparatuses, work together, position properly.

Damage. Immediately report or repair damage to the facility or to art objects.

Extinguishing flame. Use split-wind method or snuffer. Always rehearse extinguishing.

Fabric. Is it too slippery to be walked on? Flowing too close to candles? Too plush to support tabletop objects? Does it risk entanglement with ritual movement or with microphone cords?

Glue. Be especially careful with hot glue. Be mindful of the surfaces, security, and removal. Consider semi-permanent adhesives such as concealed strips of Velcro.

Helium. Obtain permission before releasing balloons indoors. Entanglement with ceiling fans, vents, lights, rafters or sky lights can cause safety and custodial problems.

Illumination. Install art in the lighting that will be used in worship, paying attention to hot light bulbs, spot canisters, and open flame.

Janitors. Set up and clean up with care. Spare custodial staff or volunteers unnecessary surprises or potential hazards. Return all borrowed tools and equipment, and treat them with utmost respect.

Knives. Store in appropriate cases in locked cabinets. Take care of surfaces.

Lifting. Use your legs, not your back. Use wagons, dollies, and big strong people.

Mice, moths, and minute creepers. They will not think your wheat, seeds, wool, silk or other natural things are special just because they are in the worship closet. Prepare carefully and store properly.

Never. Stand on the top step of the ladder, mistake a chair or a table for a ladder, stretch just that "little bit further," or stick the scissors in your pocket for the climb up the ladder.

Open flame. Be sure it is far away from things that might catch fire. Always be sure it is fully extinguished before you leave the building.

Permission. Offering others a thorough description of your intended installation and securing their consent invites the wisdom of those who may be aware of potential problems.

Quarantine. Keep under lock and key those things that are particularly fragile, valuable, or dangerous, including oil, candles, matches, and lighters.

Ritual. Consult with worship leaders on the ritual movement of objects. Meet with participants to rehearse the movements.

Stairs. Keep walkways clear. Simulate ritual movement in and around all installations near stairs.

Turbulence. Activate all potential air currents at the time of installation, noting the effect on flame, precarious objects, and fabric. Observe the airflow from heat and air conditioning vents, ceiling fans, windows, doors, and portable circulation units.

Unfixed installation. A word of instruction in the bulletin will help keep untouchables safely untouched and intentional arrangements undisturbed for the day or the season.

Veneer. Whether solid wood, inlay, or thin veneer, all wooden surfaces must be protected and treated with care.

Wax. Pour out excess wax and trim the sides while still pliable. Allow wax to cool before storing it. Do not allow debris to accumulate in the wax pool; it can act as a second wick.

Xylophones and shared space. Consult with the worship leaders on what and who will share space with the visual art. Coordinate these necessary elements to ensure safe movement and visual order.

Young ones. Consult with the worship leaders on how children will be engaged in worship and with the art in particular. Suggest how children might participate safely and freely.

Zzz. Sleeping in church can be a safety issue depending on the elbows beside you!

Candle Care

Storage

- A dry, dim, and cool place.
- Never in direct sunlight, under harsh spots, or in extreme temperatures, lest your candles fade or warp.
- Tapers should be stored horizontally and only with like-colored candles.
- Pillars should be stored upright and should not be touching other candles.

New candles

- Trim the wick to ¼ inch (5 mm) and straighten.
- New pillar candles need special care. They should be lit for one hour for every inch in diameter so that there is time for the pool of wax to spread to the farthest edge of the candle. This will leave you with an evenly burning candle without a deep valley in the center.

Keeping things tidy

- Fingerprints, scratches, and dust can be polished away with a light touch and a piece of nylon fabric.
- As a pillar burns down, pay attention to the outer rim. While the candle is still warm and pliable, gently curl the rim inward and toward the wick.
- Use glass candle rings with tapers unless you know they truly are dripless.
- Spilled wax can be removed from fabric by at least two methods. Let it harden, then cover with unwaxed brown paper and gently press it over the spot with a warm iron. Or if the fabric is washable, scrape off the excess hardened wax and run boiling water through the fabric to remove the rest.

If your candle is a smoker

- Candles burn at their best between 65 and 85 degrees F (18 to 29 degrees C). They may burn in unexpected ways outside this norm.
- Wicks should be upright and trimmed at ¼ inch (5 mm) long. Trimming should be done every time candles are extinguished. Scented candles are especially prone to smoking without careful attention to the wick.
- Avoid strong drafts or vibration to keep candles from burning too quickly or unevenly, and to avoid smoking.
- If, in spite of all your efforts, the inside of your pillar candle becomes sooty, check the length and position of the wick and wipe it clean.
- If a wick keeps smoking after you extinguish the candle, the wick is still burning and will turn to ash that won't burn well next time you light the candle. Carefully pinch the wick.

Staying safe

- Once you have read the label of a new candle (and you should read it), remove it before lighting the candle.
- Burn candles only in containers designed for that purpose. Other containers may not be sufficiently tempered.
- Make sure candles are firmly and safely seated on non-flammable holders properly sized for the candles.
- Dispose of candles when they are within one inch of the base.
- Remove all match bits, wick trimmings, or other debris from the candles.
- Maintain at least two feet of vertical clearance between a burning candle and any other surface. Make doubly sure that no other material might catch a draft and come near the open flame.
- Never blow on candles directly to extinguish them. Use a snuffer or blow gently through your fingers to avoid splattering wax on other surfaces and materials.
- Never leave an open flame unattended.

Oil candles

- An oil candle is a good choice for a candle that is always present, such as a Christ candle or a Peace candle.
- Be sure to read carefully the instructions that come with a new oil candle.

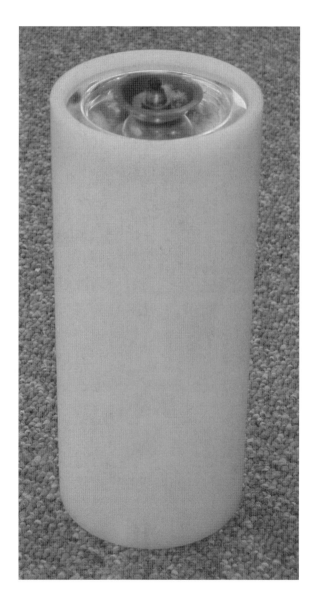

- A wick height of about an eighth of an inch (2.5 mm) will provide a good flame. Once you have this adjusted, you need not worry about trimming. Wicks are fiberglass and do not burn down. It is the oil vapor that burns, not the wick.
- Use only the lamp oil recommended.
- Do not overfill the candle. Three quarters full is usually good.
- Use a match or butane lighter to light an oil candle. Using a lighted wax candle could result in wax blocking the wick.
- Extinguish an oil candle as you would a wax candle, but be sure not to use a snuffer that has been used for wax candles.
- Clean the candle with a soft cloth.

Cleaning the Closet

Now and then we must throw open the closet door and face decisions about what stays and what must go. We dread this at home, but the task is even more daunting when it's the worship closet. At home we know the origins of items and who to consult about items we believe should be tossed. We are confident about our authority to make decisions and act on them. We can even press members of the household into service, making them responsible for their own items and sharing the work of cleaning and straightening. If only things could be that clear in the worship closet!

Does anyone know what this is?

The best way to clean the worship closet is to be careful about what is put into it in the first place and to have clearly marked containers or areas for things that are stored there.

- Stackable, clear plastic boxes work well for things you use repeatedly.
- Put like things together.
- Things that are used only once a year need to be accessible, but not front and center.
- If it's falling apart, throw it out.

Does anyone know where this came from?

In every worship closet lurk those things for which no one can account, leaving it to guesswork as to who made them, or what the intrinsic value might be. With old bulletins or pop cans, the decision to throw away is clear. But for more valuable things, find alternatives to simply putting them back where you found them.

- When the worship closet becomes a dumping ground—from a florist's column used at a recent wedding, to tinfoil wings from last year's Christmas program, to items found in the sanctuary just before worship—if they are not part of the worship closet inventory, call their owners and arrange a time for pick up.
- Some items may have historic significance in the life of the congregation. The hand

We put up signs that say, "Please put it back in an orderly way," but after a time, it will be a shambles again. Clear labeling may also help them put things back where they found them.

—LaVerle Schrag
Hutchinson, Kansas

If you don't like something you've done—even if you have put money into it—get rid of it so there's no temptation to use it again. There is nothing economical about using something that doesn't work.

—Esther Kreider Eash
Wichita, Kansas

embroidered communion drape may have been done by a founding member or the great grandmother of current members. Before you dispose of items in this category, do some careful, tactful work:

› Ask those most apt to know—former members of the worship committee, long-time members of the congregation, or the church secretary.
› Arrange the items on a table, possibly along with photos or scrapbooks. Do not mark them as items slated for disposal! Invite the congregation to reminisce. Then, listen carefully.
› If items seem to have historical significance, try to document their source and importance, then determine the best way and place to preserve them.
› If an item appears to have been a gift of considerable expense, a memorial, or an item that belonged to a family in the congregation, talk with the donor or the family of the donor.

Has anyone seen that . . . that thing?

Unless the worship closet is housed in an old bank vault or accessible to only one or two people with a key, others in the congregation may see the worship closet as a gold mine. Worship drapes can look a lot like tablecloths or breadbasket liners. That set of four expensive, matched candles won't look the same at the start of Advent if one has been used to melting crayons.

• Use signs and labels to help people put things back the way they found them.
• Label one shelf "for general use" to take the pressure off things you really don't want touched.
• If you are willing to loan from the closet, create definite, clear, and concise guidelines. Who is the contact? What is available for loan? What are the restrictions? When must it be back?
• Some things are special or unique and cannot be replaced. If the grief or guilt you imagine over the loss of such an item is great, the worship closet is probably not the place for it. Leave a note or card in the closet where it would normally be found.

These issues are even more pronounced if it is not possible for your church to have a central worship closet and worship items need to be stored in nooks and crannies all over the church. In this case, ask how you can best store your things. Can any of the spaces be better adapted with shelves or racks, better lighting, or a door? What about temperature control, dust, dampness? Proximity to high traffic areas? What things are most often used on short notice? What are some non-prime places where seasonal items can be stored? Once you have decided what will go where, label the spaces, and make a chart of each space to guide those who need to know.

Does anyone remember how we did this last time?

Some items in the closet will go unnoticed or unused for long periods of time, which means that people will forget how the items are to be used. Establish a regular routine to keep the closet useable and your materials in good condition.

- Take a few moments at your committee meeting to pick up and straighten.
- After major seasons take time to make decisions. If the items are new, assign them a place—if you are keeping them. If they are from your collection, make sure they are clean and dry before you store them. Remove candle wax or oil stains now. Are those candles too tired or burned down? Throw them out. Did you borrow something? Return it now.
- Put an annual evaluation and cleaning time on the calendar.
- Deal with those things that are your responsibility. Inquire concerning gray areas.
- Be firm, yet gentle, about what you are able to house for others.

Found Art, Shared Art

Recipe

1 Hula-Hoop	1 small "S" hook
1 large and floral ring	1 roll of fishing line
1 small florist ring	

Some assembly was required, but these items became the superstructure of a 15-foot high starfall for Advent. With the exception of the Hula-Hoop, each of these components was scavenged or recycled. The project illustrated the fact that, while costs are associated with doing visual art for worship, it is often possible to save your meager budget for that "perfect" fabric or special item that does cost money. Here are some tips to help make the most of resources that cost little or no money:

Check what's already on the shelf in the worship closet

Visuals you have already used can often be recycled with some adaptation or by using components. Try this exercise: Pull some lengths of fabric, several candles and holders, and two or three other items from the worship closet. Now, think your way through the Christian year. What possibilities lie in front of you?

If you shop, consider inexpensive options

• Begin your fabric search on the closeout or discount table. You won't always find what you are looking for, but you might. And look beyond felt. Burlap, scrim, and netting come in wide widths and are inexpensive. Subtle prints will often read as texture from even a short distance.

• Hidden components can be found in some of the most unusual places. Hula-Hoops, cooling racks, acrylic memento boxes, and dowels are examples of items that have been used in surprising and hidden ways.

- Long rolls of paper in a variety of colors, can be found at party or educator supply stores. Paper is inexpensive and can be used in many ways. Tissue paper can be extremely versatile.

Beg and borrow
- Let your needs be known in the congregation. Someone may have access to the item you need.
- Check into borrowing or renting special pieces from a local store. If there is a Ten Thousand Villages or other fair trade store in your area, for example, stop in and see what might be possible.
- Some businesses are willing to let you have remnants of raw materials.
- Consider how rock, natural woods, and indigenous plants might play a part.

Share with others
Even the most remote congregation is not alone. There are ways you may be able to share resources with other congregations in your town or district. Even at the denominational level, resources are sometimes available via the Internet or in print form.
- The Resource Library of the Western District Conference (Mennonite Church USA) in Newton, Kansas, for example, has a banner registry with pictures of banners done by area churches. Some visitors look through the file for ideas for their own designs in their congregation. Others make arrangements to borrow a banner from the host congregation.
- If you live in an area where several congregations are in close proximity, get in touch with the work they do. Share newsletters. Develop informal relationships with those involved in the visual arts in other congregations, and borrow among yourselves. Establish an annual "share and learn" event where you can share pictures, stories, learn "tricks of the trade," and bounce ideas off one another. Don't be afraid to arrange and host the first event in your area.
- Documentation is important. Pictures, design notes and other documentation of your worship centers, banners, environmental installations, communion service set-ups, and visuals are important ways to share ideas among congregations. This documentation is important in your work in the congregation, but it is also a valuable resource for sharing with others who are working to proclaim the good news through the visual arts.

For Smaller Gatherings

Worship at the heart

Sunday morning worship is the center of our life together as the body of Christ, but it's not the only opportunity to lift our hearts to the God we praise. The rhythm of congregational life includes some combination of committees meetings, commissions, councils, circles, small groups, cell groups, Bible studies, prayer groups, Sunday school classes, and midweek activities, as well as occasions that call for smaller, more intimate services. Whatever the gathering, it is right to center it in worship. Attention to the space and the visual setting plays an important role.

At meetings

Whether at a monthly committee meeting, a council retreat, or the annual congregational meeting, visuals can be as simple as:

- a candle lit to remind those gathered that Christ is present as they worship and work
- a key symbol used in Sunday worship or one that has become important in the work of the group meeting
- a ritual action that invites participation and reflection

In the classroom

- *For children:* Age appropriate and simple symbols, such as a candle, story figures, or special objects, can help children enter more fully into the story.
- *For youth:* Typically, their classroom walls are covered with posters, boards, or murals for experiments in self-expression, and the youth sit on garage-sale easy chairs. A candle or small worship center in the middle of the circle will call the youth to worship.

- *For adult learners:* While the coffee carafe may be the visual focus of fellowship, a simple worship center can help to realign focus, open hearts and minds to God, and express the teacher's care for those in the class.

Smaller services

Many communities have an established rhythm of special services (or special elements within a larger service) through the course of the year. Here are some stories of how visual art can play an important role in smaller and more intimate settings:

- **Ash Wednesday.** One church used small crosses—one of them a twig that had grown in the shape of a cross—as the visual element for an Ash Wednesday service. The use of black, the ashes, and the cross helped people enter into the tone of the service and into reflection on their lives and their mortality.
- **Service of Remembrance.** The leaders prepared a worship center that included a neutral drape over boxes of various heights, the Christ candle, a bowl of dried roses and wheat, and an informal arrangement of dried flowers and grasses in a simple crock. In the service, worshippers placed on the worship center a remembrance of a loved one who had died. In the silence that followed, as people focused on the worship center, someone in the group raised a quiet request for stories about the mementos. This led to a sacred time of storytelling, laughter, tears, healing, and community in the presence of the God we praise.
- **Welcoming New Members.** The visual artists introduced a unique and special wall hanging, a weaving of generous lengths of fabric of many colors and textures—some solid, some print, woven through a foundation of plastic construction mesh. Each new member, upon being welcomed into the congregation, chose a length of cloth from a large basket to weave into the tapestry, a reminder to all that each member of the congregation adds color and texture, and that it is through Jesus Christ that all are woven to become community.

Tips for smaller services

- Small round tables with detachable legs are easy to store and assemble when needed for smaller settings. A corresponding collection of round tablecloths in the colors of the liturgical year will help you be ready for each season.
- A tall, freestanding candle stand for a Christ candle can be used for a council meeting, retreat setting, congregational meeting, or small service.

- In smaller settings you can use votives, tea lights, or floating candles effectively in ways that would be lost on Sunday morning.
- Black and white photographs are inexpensive and can be extremely effective in small settings.
- Smaller services are your opportunity to use those pieces that you have gathered over time but are not large enough to be used in Sunday worship.

Tips for helping others work at visuals for their meetings

- Make a shelf in the worship closet available to committees and classes. Include simple candle holders; collected candles that are perfectly good, but too burned down for Sunday worship; and small, interesting pieces of cloth, such as an assortment of cloth napkins in various colors.
- At the beginning of the new year, offer a mini-workshop for council, commission, and committee chairs, and Sunday school teachers, to let them know about the shelf, to encourage them to think about using visual elements, and to give them quick and easy tips to get them started.
- Always model the use of visual elements when the meeting or class is your responsibility.

Cautions

Designs that impede engagement with Scripture

Idolatry. Visual art does not pretend to be God any more than does a sermon. Like some sermons, visual art proclaims God's presence in metaphorical ways. God is not a rock, a hen, or a shepherd—but through such imagery we recognize God as protective, nurturing, and guiding. Just as verbal metaphors are used throughout the Bible, visual metaphors have an important place in our worship. They can only become idols if we make them so.

Showcasing. Worship is an altar, not an easel. In humble service, we offer to God the arts of preaching, quilting, gardening, and carpentry. If engagement with art stops at the art itself then it has failed to do what liturgy intends—to point beyond itself to the gospel of Christ.

Prescription. The difference between prescriptive and descriptive art is the difference between telling us what to see and showing us how to look. Acts' vivid description of flaming tongues and songs like "Holy Spirit, come with power," make calligraphing "Alleluia" on a crimson banner a little redundant. The red itself proclaims the Spirit's presence, power, and call.

Pedagogy. Imagery is a valued tool for teaching, but in worship, images are principally about formation, not information. A banner installation can function liturgically as a piece that leads people to pray, centers us in time, or evokes scriptural engagement. But in misplaced pragmatism, it can be little more than an adult-sized flannel board.

Domesticity. In a home, artwork reflects the tastes of the family. Worship, however, is a public, corporate act. In the corporate family of faith, worship art needs to be "big enough" in meaning and intent for that gathered body. In the context of worship the least desirable thing is art "too small" to encompass corporate meaning, too anaesthetizing to maintain engagement with the Word.

Where a sense of genuine beauty is lost, the good also loses its force of attraction; and where goodness no longer attracts, beauty becomes a shadow of itself.

—*William A. Dyrness*
Visual Faith

I think if I could wish something for many of the visuals I'm part of it's that people can interact with them at many different levels, engage at different levels—just like any other part of the worship service. Somehow it meets people right where they are.

—*Esther Kreider Eash*
Wichita, Kansas

Our hope is to let the visuals evoke instead of try to teach.

—*Todd Friesen*
Lombard, Illinois

I am no more likely to explain [the visual] in the bulletin than I am to explain why we pray, what we're singing, or what the sermon is beforehand.

— *Lois Siemens*
Kerrobert, Saskatchewan

Aesthetics. Likewise, art in the worship space, as the carrier of corporate meaning, must not be mistaken for mere decoration. Story dwells in symbol. Journey is marked in the colors of the Christian year. Merely decorative choices, however, live in the momentary trend and will not bear the weight of the gospel.

Ugly, misunderstood. Art that carries meaning may well not be pretty. Art in worship can carry the weight of ugliness and be dissonant because it is set in the liturgy, in the layers of worship, which carry alternative forms of hope and reconciliation. It can become an emblem of truth and beauty.

Art that has to be explained. Though we might be tempted to explain the art we do for worship, our task is to invite conversation with the art. Explaining more often closes off conversation than begins it. The place of art in worship is to evoke, and evocation opens the possibility of multiple meanings and simultaneous interactions at many levels.

Evangelism. Proclamation of the gospel is our Great Commission. If the gathered are invited to apprehend, participate, and respond, then the good news, compelling and winsome, has been rightly proclaimed. Coercion or manipulation can become a powerful temptation. We must remember that the outcomes of that proclamation rest solely with God.

Entertainment. While the gospel is winsome, it is not entertainment. Entertainment is passive and titillating, making no demands of its audience. The arts of worship exist to proclaim, to invite full-being participation and response to the God we praise. In these arts lies a call to rehabituate ourselves into a sacramental worldview and into holiness.

Evaluation

The Artist's Prayer—
Ephesians 3:14-21

This tool, based on Paul's prayer for the congregation at Ephesus, offers worship planners and artists an evaluative tool in the Trinitarian model. It's best to start by determining which of three primary functions the art has in worship: leading worship, fostering community, or inspiring community. Once you have answered that question, consult the objectives listed for the category to gauge the visual effect. If visual art is properly supported by other elements of worship, it does not need to perform all three functions. Another way to use the evaluation tool is simply to consult the objectives in each of the three categories and answer one or two of the questions.

Worship criteria

For this reason I bow my knees before God . . .

- Does the art reveal God's face, God's character, or God's Kingdom desires?
- Does it illumine the Scripture text or the season's theological meaning?
- Does it inspire or enable prayer?
- Does it lead to authentic praise or honest lament?
- Does it call forth confession, having shown us and our world to be flawed?
- Does it assure us of the Good News of forgiveness, reconciliation, and peace?
- Is it properly installed in the liturgy, supported by other functions of worship?
- Does it visually evoke an "amen"?

Community criteria

. . . from whom every family in heaven and on earth takes its name . . .

- Does the art reveal something about Jesus, his divinity, humanity, or mission?
- Does it remind the congregation of a story fundamental to the faith tradition?
- Is it free of cliché, prescription, and moralistic imagery?
- Are people free to interpret for themselves and as a community?
- Does it unify the perspective, character, and conduct of the church?
- Does it remind the congregation of its core identity?
- Does it affirm the congregation's identity with symbols that are deeply rooted and relevant to the congregation's life?
- Does it invite participation across lines of age, race, gender, and background?
- Does it create a sense of unity and compassion for one another and the world?

Mission criteria

. . . so to him who by the power at work within us is able to
accomplish abundantly more than all we can ask or imagine . . .

- Does the art reveal something about the presence and purpose of the Holy Spirit?
- Does it summon a response for mission, service, evangelism, or peace-making?
- Does it inspire a more ethical way of believing and behaving?
- Does it inspire individual growth and personal devotion?
- Does it confront cultural ideals? offer a prophetic rebuke? subvert dominant patterns?
- Does it call forth an imaginative response to the Kingdom of God?
- Does it send us with a renewed sense of zeal and commitment?

To God be the glory in the church and in Christ Jesus
to all generations, forever and ever. Amen.

How feedback comes

- **Observing the congregation in the moment of worship.** This is the art of corporate pastoral care. Are the people saying amen, either verbally or through their level of engagement? Do the eyes of those involved in ritual movement reveal that more is going on than the outward action? Become competent facilitators of corporate visual encounter.

Proclamation—Declaring, revealing, showing, demonstrating. The art of bringing the story forward to mix with our story, inviting congregational participation, conversation, and response.

Ritual—A melding of words and action that brings sacrament to life and situates it in the biblical Story and in our ongoing story.

Sacrament—An action that Jesus put into place and holds within it the promise of his presence.

Sponsoring faith—Pastoral care given to the faith-shaping designs of worship through the tools of story and ritual, acknowledging that God is the one who forms God's people.

Symbol—Something that is recognized to carry meaning and points beyond itself to the substance of that meaning.

Theology—Eyes wide open and expecting to see God. Thinking, talking, and acting on the basis of God's ongoing interaction in the world.

Transcendent—Beyond and greater than the limits of the material world.

Trinity/Holy Trinity—Threeness. God, Jesus, Holy Spirit, three in one, one in three.

Vocation—That to which God calls us. It may or may not be the same as one's occupation.

Worship—The corporate experience of praising God for no other reason than that God is worthy of our praise.

Notes

Chapter 1
The God We Praise

1. The term *revelation*, as we use it, should be read with a small "r." It is the fruit of doing theology—the insights we bring to the assembly for consideration and testing. It is not to be confused with Scripture or the Incarnation of Christ, which constitute the large "R" Revelation.

2. The classical term used by scholars to describe this community is *perichoresis*. Daniel Migliore provides a very helpful definition: "the passing into one another—indwell each other, make room for each other, incomparably hospitable" (*Faith Seeking Understanding: An Introduction to Christian Theology*. Grand Rapids: Eerdmans, 1991, 70).

3. Marlene Kropf, "How Do We Know When It's Good Worship?" *Vision: a Journal for Church and Theology* 6 (Fall 2005): 40.

4. Lois Siemens, interview, n.d.

5. Lynette Wiebe, interview, August 2005.

6. Author's recollection, Hope Mennonite Church, Wichita, Kansas, Ordinary time 2006.

7. Brian Wren, *Praying Twice: the Music and Words of Congregational Song* (Louisville: Westminster John Knox, 2000), 361.

8. Marilyn Houser Hamm, *Hymnal: A Worship Book* (Newton, KS: Faith and Life Press, 1992), 20.

9. Elouise Renich Fraser, *Confessions of a Beginning Theologian* (Downers Grove, IL: InterVarsity Press, 1998), 92.

10. "Limiting the term 'Word of God' to its written form blinds us to the total witness of Scripture." *Confession of Faith in a Mennonite Perspective* (Scottdale, PA: Herald Press, 1995), 23.

11. Walter Klaassen, "Biblical and Theological Bases for Worship in the Believer's Church," *Worship Series* No. 1 (Newton, KS: Faith and Life Press, 1983): 14.

12. Michael Moynahan, "Liturgy, Arts, and Spirituality," *Liturgical Ministry* 5 (Summer 1996): 108-20 cited in Doug Adams and Michael E. Moynahan, *Postmodern Worship and the Arts* (San Jose, CA: Resource Publications, Inc., 2002), 140.

13. Robin M Jensen, *The Substance of Things Seen: Art, Faith, and the Christian Community* (Grand Rapids: Eerdmans, 2004), 73.

14. Barbara Brown Taylor, *The Preaching Life* (Cambridge: Cowley Publications, 1993), 45.

15. Jean Janzen, "Why We are Afraid of Art," *Direction* 27 (Fall 1998): 123.

Chapter 2
The Scripture We Proclaim

1. Mark 10:13-16. Author paraphrase.
2. Robin R Meyers, *With Ears to Hear: Preaching as Self-Persuasion* (Cleveland: The Pilgrim Press, 1993), 90.
3. Ibid.
4. Tom F. Driver, *The Magic of Ritual: Our Need for Liberating Rites that Transform Our Lives and Our Communities* (San Francisco: HarperCollins, 1991), 214.
5. John Rempel, "Ritual is My Third Language: An Autobiographical Account," *Mennonite Quarterly Review* 79 (January 2005): 8-9.
6. Ibid., 16.
7. Pam Driedger, "In the Ordinary, Glimpses of the Extraordinary," *Vision: A Journal for Church and Theology* 6 (Fall 2005): 17.
8. Bruce C. Burch, "The Arts, Midrash, and Biblical Teaching," in *Arts, Theology, & The Church: New Intersections*, Kimberly Vrudny and Wilson Yates, eds. (Cleveland: The Pilgrim Press, 2005), 108.
9. Ibid., 109.
10. Klaassen, "Biblical and Theological Bases for Worship in the Believer's Church," 14.
11. *Confession of Faith in a Mennonite Perspective*, 22.
12. Lois Siemens, interview, n.d.
13. William A. Dyrness. *Visual Faith: Art, Theology, and Worship in Dialogue* (Grand Rapids, Michigan: Baker Academic, 2001), 85.
14. Esther Kreider Eash, interview, January 2005.

Chapter 3
The Design We Offer

1. Marlene Kropf, "Worship: Ceremony, Symbol, and Celebration" (lecture, Associated Mennonite Biblical Seminary, Elkhart, IN, June 2000).
2. *Confession of Faith in a Mennonite Perspective*, 22.
3. Duane Beck, statement during worship at Belmont Mennonite Church, Elkhart, IN, n.d.
4. Lois Siemens, interview, n.d.
5. Author's recollection, Belmont Mennonite Church, Elkhart, IN, Good Shepherd Sunday, n.d.
6. Robin R. Meyers, *With Ears to Hear* (Cleveland: Pilgrim Press, 1993), 3.
7. Ibid., 45.
8. Clayton J. Schmit, *Too Deep for Words* (Louisville: Westminster John Knox Press, 2002), 9, 85.
9. Joe Loganbill, interview, May 2005.
10. Marylou Weaver Houser, interview, April 2006.
11. Karen Stone, *Image and Spirit* (Minneapolis: Augsburg Books, 2003), 115.
12. Nancy Chinn, *Spaces for Spirit* (Chicago: Liturgy Training Publications, 1989), 2.
13. Ibid., 24.
14. The tradition that has assigned the use of specific colors in the seasons of the liturgical year is a long one and is followed by Christians of all cultures. At the same time, we must acknowledge that the

color black has sometimes been taken to perpetuate the racist attitude that associates people with black skin with sin and darkness, and people with white skin with purity or light. Some churches respond to this awareness by avoiding the traditional colors of the liturgical year altogether, or simply forgo the use of black on Good Friday. Others, including liturgical churches within the African-American community, follow the tradition and accept the original theological intent of the colors.

15. Meyers, *With Ears to Hear*, 89.
16. Ibid.
17. These are summarized in a chart on page 94. The chart, inspired by previously unpublished material by Karmen Krahn, is also used in *Preparing Sunday Dinner* by June Alliman Yoder, Marlene Kropf, and Rebecca Slough (Scottdale, PA: Herald Press, 2005), 265.
18. Alliman Yoder, et.al., 266.
19. This category, "the representational," is identified in many art theory texts as "figurative."
20. Author's recollection, Associated Mennonite Biblical Seminary, n.d.
21. Mary Lou Weaver Houser, interview, April 2006.
22. Ibid.
23. Jane Peifer, correspondence, June 2005.
24. This category, "the universal," is identified in many art theory texts as "abstract."
25. Barbara Peterson, correspondence, November 2006.

Chapter 4
The People We Become

1. Rodney A. Clapp, *A Peculiar People: the Church as Culture in a Post-Christian Society* (Downer's Grove, IL: InterVarsity Press, 1996), 116.
2. Alan Kreider, *Worship and Evangelism in Pre-Christendom* (Cambridge, UK: Grove Books Limited, 1995), 24.
3. Ibid., 25.
4. Ibid.
5. Rempel, "Ritual is My Third Language: An Autobiographical Account," 9.
6. Kreider, *Worship and Evangelism in Pre-Christendom*, 33.
7. Doug Luginbill, interview, March 2005.
8. Deb Schmidt, interview, February 2005.
9. Alan Kreider, lecture, Associated Mennonite Biblical Seminary, n.d.
10. Clapp, *A Peculiar People*, 118.

Recommended Readings for the Studio

Heart

Boers, Arthur Paul. *On Earth as In Heaven: Justice Rooted in Spirituality.* Waterloo, ON: Herald Press, 1991.

Chinn, Nancy. *Spaces for Spirit: Adorning the Church.* Chicago: Liturgy Training Publications, 1989.

Dillard, Annie. *Teaching a Stone to Talk: Expeditions and Encounters.* New York: Harper and Row, 1982.

Duck, Ruth. *Finding Words for Worship: A Guide for Leaders.* Louisville, KY: Westminster John Knox, 1995.

Gerding, Jeri. *Drawing to God: Art as Prayer, Prayer as Art.* Notre Dame, IN: Sorin Books, 2001.

Jensen, Robin M. *The Substance of Things Seen: Art, Faith, and the Christian Community.* Grand Rapids: Eerdmans, 2004.

Kapikian, Catherine, and Kathleen Black. *Art in Service of the Sacred: Symbol and Design for Worship Spaces.* Nashville: Abingdon, 2006.

Lawrence, Kenneth T., et al. *Imaging the Word: An Arts and Lectionary Resource.* 3 vols. Cleveland: United Church Press, 1992.

L'Engle, Madeleine. *Walking on Water: Reflections on Faith and Art.* Wheaton, IL: H. Shaw, 1980.

McCollough, Charles with the poetry of Maren Tirabassi. *Faith Made Visible: Shaping the Human Spirit in Sculpture and Word.* Cleveland, OH: United Church Press, 2000.

Meyers, Robin R. *With Ears to Hear: Preaching as Self-Persuasion.* Cleveland: The Pilgrim Press, 1993.

Pope John Paul II. *Letter to Artists.* Chicago: Liturgy Training Publications, 1999.

Oswald, Roy M. *Transforming Rituals: Daily Practices for Changing Lives.* Bethesda, MD: Alban Institute, 1999.

Reimer, Margaret Loewen. "Mennonites and the Artistic Imagination." *Conrad Grebel Review* 16 (Fall 1998): 6-24.

Willimon, William H. *Worship as Pastoral Care.* Nashville: Abingdon, 1979.

Yoder, John Howard. *Body Politics: Five Practices of the Christian Community Before the Watching World.* Nashville, TN: Discipleship Resources, 1992.

Head

Allen, Horace T. *A Handbook for the Lectionary.* Philadelphia: Geneva Press, 1980.

Anderson, Herbert. *Mighty Stories, Dangerous Rituals: Weaving Together the Human and the Divine.* San Francisco: Jossey-Bass, 1998.

Begbie, Jeremy, ed. *Beholding the Glory: Incarnation Through the Arts.* Grand Rapids, MI: Baker Books, 2000.

Begbie, Jeremy. *Voicing Creation's Praise: Towards a Theology of the Arts.* Edinburgh: T&T Clark, 1991.

Bryans, Nena. *Full Circle: A Proposal to the Church for an Arts Ministry.* San Jose, California: Schuyler Institute for Worship and the Arts, 1988. (This book has been reprinted by and available from the author. Nena Bryans, 302 Spencer Road, Devon, PA 19333-1431. (610) 644-6935.)

Chinn, Nancy. "Evaluating Visual Art for Worship." *Reformed Liturgy and Music* 23 (Summer 1989): 114-15.

DeBoer, Lisa. "Make a Vision Statement: Basics for Bringing New Life to Your Worship Visuals." *Reformed Worship,* no. 55 (March 2000): 40-42.

Driver, Tom F. *Liberating Rites: Understanding the Transforming Power of Ritual.* Boulder, CO: Westview Press, 1998.

Fee, Gordon D. and Stuart Douglas. *How to Read the Bible for All It's Worth: A Guide to Understanding the Bible.* Grand Rapids: Zondervan, 1993.

Janzen, Jean. " Why We Are Afraid of Art." *Direction* 27, no. 2 (Fall 1998): 123-31.

Jensen, Robin Margaret. *Face to Face: Portraits of the Divine in Early Christianity.* Minneapolis: Fortress Press, 2005.

Kennel, LeRoy. "Visual Arts and Worship." *Worship Series* no 14. Newton, KS: Faith and Life Press, (1983).

Klaassen, Walter. "Biblical and Theological Bases for Worship in the Believer's Church." *Worship Series,* no. 1 (1983).

Miller, Levi, ed. *The Meetinghouse of God's People.* Scottdale, PA: Mennonite Publishing House, 1977.

Saliers, Don E. *Worship Comes to Its Senses.* Nashville: Abingdon Press, 1996.

Schmit, Clayton J. *Too Deep for Words: A Theology of Liturgical Expression.* Louisville: Westminster John Knox, 2002.

Simons, Thomas G. and James M. Fitzpatrick. *The Ministry of Liturgical Environment.* Collegeville, MI: The Liturgical Press, 1984.

Skudlarek, William. *The Word in Worship: Preaching in a Liturgical Context.* Nashville: Abingdon, 1981.

Stone, Karen. *Image and Spirit: Finding Meaning in Visual Art.* Minneapolis: Augsburg Books, 2003.

Voska, Richard S. *Designing Future Worship Spaces: The Mystery of a Common Vision.* Chicago: Liturgy Training Publications, 1966.

Yoder, June Alliman, Marlene Kropf, and Rebecca Slough. *Preparing Sunday Dinner: A Collaborative Approach to Worship and Preaching.* Scottdale, PA: Herald Press, 2005.

Webber, Robert E., ed. "Music and the Visual Arts in Christian Worship," *The Complete Library of Christian Worship* vol. 4, books 1 and 2. Nashville, TN: Star Song Publishing Group (1994).

_____. "The Services of the Christian Year," *The Complete Library of Christian Worship,* vol. 5. Nashville, TN: Star Song Publishing Group (1994).

White, James F. and Susan J. White. *Church Architecture: Building and Renovating for Christian Worship.* Nashville, TN: Abingdon, 1998.

White, James F. *Introduction to Christian Worship.* rev. ed. Nashville: Abingdon Press, 1980.

Hand

Chinn, Nancy. *Spaces for Spirit: Adorning the Church.* Chicago: Liturgy Training Publications, 1998.

Dillaser, Maurice, ed. *The Symbols of the Church.* Collegeville, MN: The Liturgical Press, 1999.

Flachman, Leonard. *Symbol Patterns: Ideas for Banners, Posters, Bulletin Boards.* Minneapolis: Augsburg Publishing House, 1981.

Gaddy, G. Welton and Don W. Nixon. *A Symphony for the Senses: Worship Resources for Christian Congregations.* Macon, GA: Smyth & Helwys Publishing, 1995.

Kapikian, Catherine A. *Through the Christian Year: An Illustrated Guide.* Nashville: Abingdon Press, 1983.

Klein, Patricia S. *Worship Without Words: The Signs and Symbols of Our Faith.* Brewster, MA: Paraclete Press, 2000.

Kreider, Eleanor. *Communion Shapes Character.* Scottdale, PA: Herald Press, 1997.

Morton, Craig and Ken Hawkley. *Word of Mouth: Creative Ways to Present Scripture.* Newton, KS: Faith & Life Press, 2000.

Philippart, David, ed. *Clothed in Glory: Vesting the Church.* Chicago: Liturgy Training Publications, 1997.

Rosser, Aelred R. *A Well-Trained Tongue: Formation in the Ministry of a Reader.* Chicago: Liturgy Training Publications, 1996.

_____. *A World That Will Rouse Them: Reflections on the Ministry of a Reader.* Chicago: Liturgy Training Publications, 1995.

Websites

www.civa.org CIVA: Christians in the Visual Arts: Connecting the Artist, the Church and the Culture.

www.churcharts.org Imago Dei: Friends of Christianity and the Arts.

www.leaderonline.org The online companion to "Leader: Equipping the Missional Church," a quarterly magazine for pastors and lay leaders in Anabaptist congregations.

www.mennoniteusa.org OneSource: An Online Resource Network.

www.shindigz.com Shindigz by Stumps: World's Largest Party Superstore. A good source for roll paper and gossamer in many colors.

Bibliography
of Works Cited
and Consulted

Adams, Doug and Michael E. Moynahan, ed. *Postmodern Worship and the Arts.* San Jose, CA: Resource Publications, Inc., 2002.

Allen, Pamela Payne. "Creativity and the Challenge of Worship." *Christian Century* 104 (September 9-16, 1987): 756-58.

Begbie, Jeremy, ed. *Beholding the Glory: Incarnation through the Arts.* Grand Rapids: Baker Books, 2000.

Begbie, Jeremy. *Voicing Creation's Praise: Towards a Theology of the Arts.* Edinburgh: T&T Clark, 1991.

Brown, Barbara Taylor. *The Preaching Life.* Cambridge: Cowley Publications, 1993.

Chinn, Nancy. "Evaluating Visual Art for Worship." *Reformed Liturgy and Music* 23 (Summer 1989): 114-15.

Chinn, Nancy. *Spaces for Spirit: Adorning the Church.* Chicago: Liturgy Training Publications, 1989.

Clapp, Rodney. *A Peculiar People: the Church as Culture in a Post-Christian Society.* Downer's Grove, IL: InterVarsity Press, 1996.

Confession of Faith in a Mennonite Perspective. Scottdale, PA and Waterloo, ON: Herald Press, 1995.

Driedger, Pam. "In the Ordinary, Glimpses of the Extraordinary." *Vision: A Journal for Church and Theology* 6 (Fall 2005): 14-20.

Driver, Tom F. *The Magic of Ritual: Our Need for Liberating Rites that Transform Our Lives and Our Communities.* San Francisco: HarperCollins, 1991.

Dyrness, William A. *Visual Faith: Art, Theology, and Worship in Dialogue.* Grand Rapids, MI: Baker Books, 2001.

Eusden, John D. and John H. Westerhoff. *Sensing Beauty: Aesthetics, the Human Spirit, and the Church.* Cleveland: United Church Press, 1998.

Fraser, Elouise Renich. *Confessions of a Beginning Theologian.* Downer's Grove, IL: InterVarsity Press, 1998.

Friesen, Duane K. *Artists, Citizens, Philosophers: Seeking the Peace of the City.* Scottdale, PA: Herald Press, 2000.

Irvine, Christopher and Anne Dawtry. *Art and Worship.* Collegeville, MN: Liturgical Press, 2002.

Janzen, Jean. "Why We are Afraid of Art." *Direction* 27, no. 2 (Fall 1998): 123-31.

Janzen, Reinhild Kauenhoven. "Door to the Spiritual: The Visual Arts in Anabaptist-Mennonite Worship." *Mennonite Quarterly Review* 73, no. 2 (April 1999): 367-90.

Jensen, Robin M. *The Substance of Things Seen: Art, Faith, and the Christian Community.* Grand Rapids: Eerdmans, 2004.

Kennel, LeRoy. "Visual Arts and Worship." *Worship Series,* no. 14. Newton, KS: Faith and Life Press (1983).

Klaassen, Walter. "Biblical and Theological Bases for Worship in the Believer's Church." *Worship Series,* no. 1. Newton, KS: (1983).

Kreider, Alan. *Worship and Evangelism in Pre-Christendom.* Cambridge, UK: Grove Books Limited, 1995.

Kropf, Marlene. "How Do We Know When It's Good Worship?" *Vision: A Journal for Church and Theology* 6 (Fall 2005): 36-44.

Lathrop, Gordon W. *Holy Things: A Liturgical Theology.* Minneapolis: Fortress Press, 1993.

Meyers, Robin R. *With Ears to Hear: Preaching as Self-Persuasion.* Cleveland: The Pilgrim Press, 1993.

Moeller, Pamela Ann. *Exploring Worship Anew: Dreams and Visions.* St. Louis: Chalice Press, 1998.

National Conference of Catholic Bishops, Bishops' Committee on the Liturgy, *Environment & Art in Catholic Worship.* Chicago: Liturgy Training Publications, 1978.

Placher, William C. *Narratives of a Vulnerable God: Christ, Theology, and Scripture.* Louisville: Westminster John Knox, 1994.

Pope John Paul II. *Letter to Artists*. Chicago: Liturgy Training Publications, 1999.

Power, David Noel. *Unsearchable Riches: The Symbolic Nature of Liturgy*. New York: Pueblo Publishing Company, 1984.

Reimer, Margaret Loewen. "Mennonites and the Artistic Imagination." *Conrad Grebel Review* 16 (Fall 1998): 6-24.

Rempel, John. "Ritual is My Third Language: An Autobiographical Account." *Mennonite Quarterly Review* 79 (January 2005): 7-18.

Rice, Charles L. *The Embodied Word: Preaching as Art and Liturgy*. Minneapolis: Fortress Press, 1991.

Saliers, Don E. "Beauty and Holiness Revisited: Some Relations between Aesthetics and Theology." *Worship* 48, no. 5 (May 1974): 278-93.

Saliers, Don E. *Worship Comes to Its Senses*. Nashville: Abingdon Press, 1996.

Saliers, Don E. *Worship as Theology: Foretaste of Glory Divine*. Nashville: Abingdon, 1994.

Schmidt, Orlando. "The Use of the Fine Arts in the Mennonite Church." Unpublished thesis, New York Biblical Seminary, 1949.

Schmit, Clayton J. *Too Deep for Words: A Theology of Liturgical Expression*. Louisville: Westminster John Knox, 2002.

Senn, Frank C. *New Creation: A Liturgical World View*. Minneapolis: Fortress Press, 2000.

Stone, Karen. *Image and Spirit: Finding Meaning in Visual Art*. Minneapolis: Augsburg Books, 2003.

Toews, A. P. *American Mennonite Worship: Its Roots, Development, and Application*. New York: Exposition Press, 1960.

Van Dyk, Leanne, ed. *A More Profound Alleluia: Theology and Worship in Harmony*. Grand Rapids: Eerdmans, 2005.

Vrudny, Kimberly and Wilson Yates, ed. *Arts, Theology and the Church: New Intersections*. Cleveland: The Pilgrim Press, 2005.

Yoder, June Alliman, Marlene Kropf, and Rebecca Slough. *Preparing Sunday Dinner: A Collaborative Approach to Worship and Preaching*. Scottdale, PA: Herald Press, 2005.

Walton, Janet R. *Art and Worship: A Vital Connection*. Wilmington, DE: Michael Glazier, Inc., 1988.

Webber, Robert E., ed. "Music and the Visual Arts in Christian Worship." *The Complete Library of Christian Worship*, vol. 4, book 2 (1994).

White, James F. *Introduction to Christian Worship.* Rev. ed. Nashville: Abingdon Press, 1980.

Wolterstorff, Nicholas. *Art in Action: Toward a Christian Aesthetic.* Grand Rapids: Eerdmans, 1980.

Wren, Brian. *Praying Twice: the Music and Words of Congregational Song.* Louisville: Westminster John Knox, 2000.

Interviews

Eash, Esther Kreider. Hope Mennonite Church. Wichita, Kansas. 22 January 2005.

Friesen, Joanna Fenton, Carol Sue Hobbs, Joe Loganbill, Eric Massanari, Chuck Regier, and Mark Wasser. Shalom Mennonite Church. Newton, Kansas. 4 May 2005.

Friesen, Todd. Lombard Mennonite Church. Lombard, Illinois. 23 March 2006.

Luginbill, Doug. Hope Mennonite Church. Wichita, Kansas. 3 March 2005.

Pinkerton, Joanna. Hope Mennonite Church. Wichita, Kansas. 31 March 2005.

Rempel, Elsie and Lynette Wiebe. Charleswood Mennonite Church, Winnipeg, Manitoba. 12 August 2005.

Schrag, LaVerle. First Mennonite Church. Hutchinson, Kansas. 18 November 2004.

Schmidt, Deb. First Mennonite Church. Hutchinson, Kansas. 22 February 2005.

Siemens, Lois. Superb Mennonite Church. Kerrobert, Saskatchewan. n.d.

Steinmann, Pauline. Wildwood Mennonite Church. Saskatoon, Saskatchewan. 10 March 2006.

Weaver Houser, Mary Lou. Community Mennonite Church. Lancaster, Pennsylvania. 23 February 2006.

Correspondence

Dick, Dorothy. Foothills Mennonite Church. Calgary, Alberta.

Friesen, Matt. Albany Mennonite Church. Albany, Oregon.

Hofer, Michelle L. Hutterthal Mennonite Church. Freeman, South Dakota.

Johnson, Norma. Bethel College Mennonite Church. Newton, Kansas.

Peterson, Barbara. Trinity Methodist Church, Elkhart, Indiana.

Peifer, Jane. Blossom Hill Mennonite Church. Lancaster, Pennsylvania.

Ringenberg, Frances. Lombard Mennonite Church. Lombard, Illinois.

Shenk, Kris. Belmont Mennonite Church. Elkhart, Indiana.

Spaulding, Randall. Covenant Mennonite Fellowship. Sarasota, Florida.

Thiessen, Lavina. Steinbach Mennonite Church. Steinbach, Manitoba.

Wenger, Tonya Ramer. Madison Mennonite Church. Madison, Wisconsin.

Yoder, Laurie. Lombard Mennonite Church. Lombard, Illinois.

Art and Photo Credits

Key: **page number**, *artist*, photographer.

Chapter 1: The God We Praise
6 *Leslie James*, LJ. **7** *Karmen Krahn*, Leslie James. **8** *Karmen Krahn*, KK. **9** *Esther Kreider Eash*, Vicki Hofer-Holdeman. **10** *Esther Kreider Eash*, Leslie James. **11** *Esther Kreider Eash*, Leslie James.

Chapter 2: The Scripture We Proclaim
19 *Karmen Krahn*, KK. **21** *Karmen Krahn*, Leslie James. **25** *LaVerle Schrag*, Leslie James. **26** *Joanna Fenton Friesen*, JFF (top). *Tonya Ramer Wenger*, TRW (bottom). **28** *Esther Kreider Eash*, Leslie James.

Chapter 3: The Design We Offer
32 *Karmen Krahn*, KK. **35** *Karmen Krahn*, Leslie James. **37** *Delores Harnish*, Mary Lou Weaver Houser (both). **38** *Karmen Krahn*, Leslie James. **39** *Advent planning group*, Tonya Ramer Wenger. **42** *Karmen Krahn*, KK. **43** *Christian Fisher*, Mary Lou Weaver Houser. **44** *Congregational art—Blossom Hill Mennonite*, Jane Peifer.

Chapter 4: The People We Become
47 *Scott Hoefer*, Leslie James. **56** *Scott Hoefer*, Leslie James. **60** *Scott Hoefer*, Leslie James.

The Catalogue
62 (Butterfly) *Katy Nissley*, Tonya Ramer Wenger. (Origami) *Joanne Juhnke*, Tonya Ramer Wenger. (Cross with blossoms, candles) *Madison Mennonite Church planning group*, Tonya Ramer Wenger. (Drawings) *Ben Bauman*, Tonya Ramer Wenger. **63** *Robert Regier*, Leslie James (both). **64, 65** *Scott Hoefer*, Leslie James (all). **66** *Karmen Krahn*, KK. *Esther Kreider Eash*, Leslie James. **67** *Laurie Yoder*, LY (both). **68** (Figures on path, spirals, flowers) *Phil Sawatzky*, Chuck Regier. (Holy Spirit, pieced cross) *Charlotte Warkentine*, Chuck Regier. **69** *Karmen Krahn*, KK (all). **70, 71** *Kris Shenk*, KS (all). **72** *Leslie James*, LJ (all). **73** *LaVerle Schrag*, Vicki Hofer Holdeman (all). **74** *Karmen Krahn*, KK (all). **75** *Esther Kreider Eash*, Leslie James (both). **76, 77** (Spirals) *Christian Fisher*, Mary Lou Weaver Houser. (Quilts) *Delores Harnish*, Mary Lou Weaver Houser. (Pentecost spiral) *Jan Siemens/Mary Lou Weaver Houser*, MLWH. (Window) *Community Mennonite Church*, Mary Lou Weaver Houser. **78** *Esther Kreider Eash*, Leslie James (all). **79** *Karmen Krahn*, KK. *Leslie James*, LJ. **80** *Hope Mennonite Church Worship Committee*, Vicki Hofer Holdeman, Leslie James. (Pitcher/bowl) *Karmen Krahn*, Leslie James. **81** *Karmen Krahn*, Leslie James (all). **82** (Lepers) *LaVerle Schrag*, Leslie James. (Rocks) *Karmen Krahn*, Leslie James. **83** Clockwise: *Karmen Krahn*, *Hope Mennonite Church worship committee*, *Karmen Krahn*, *Leslie James*, *Joanna Pinkerton*, Leslie James. **84** *Karmen Krahn*, KK (all).

The Studio
86 Vicki Hofer Holdeman. **87** *LaVerle Schrag*, Leslie James. **89** *Leslie James*, LJ. **92** *Karmen Krahn*, Leslie James. **93** *Karmen Krahn*, Leslie James. **96** *Karmen Krahn*, KK. **101** *Joanna Pinkerton*, Leslie James. **104** *Karmen Krahn*, KK. **106** *Karmen Krahn*, KK. **109** *Karmen Krahn*, Leslie James. **110** *Joanna Pinkerton*, Leslie James. **112, 113** *Leslie James*, LJ. **118** *Leslie James*, LJ. **119** *Karmen Krahn*, KK. *Phil Sawatzky*, Chuck Regier. **120** *Karmen Krahn*, KK. **121** *Esther Kreider Eash*, Karmen Krahn. *Leslie James*, LJ. **125** *LaVerle Schrag*, Vicki Hofer Holdeman.

About the Authors

Benita Struik

Karmen Krahn is a youth worker in an alternative education program in Swift Current, Saskatchewan. Besides being a spiritual director, she is also involved in the local visual and performing arts community. She has a Master of Arts in Christian Formation from Associated Mennonite Biblical Seminary in Elkhart, Indiana. She is a member of Belmont Mennonite Church in Elkhart.

Vicki Hofer-Holdeman

Leslie James lives in Wichita, Kansas, where she is a medical librarian in a major teaching hospital. She is a member of Wichita's Hope Mennonite Church where she has long been involved in worship planning, worship leading, the arts in worship, and served as an interim pastor in 2007. She is working toward a Masters of Divinity through Associated Mennonite Biblical Seminary.